THE THEORY

OF

ABSTRACT ETHICS

THE THEORY

OF

ABSTRACT ETHICS

by

THOMAS WHITTAKER

Author of *The Neo-Platonists*

Cambridge:

at the University Press

1916

CAMBRIDGE
UNIVERSITY PRESS

University Printing House, Cambridge CB2 8BS, United Kingdom

Cambridge University Press is part of the University of Cambridge.

It furthers the University's mission by disseminating knowledge in the pursuit of education, learning and research at the highest international levels of excellence.

www.cambridge.org
Information on this title: www.cambridge.org/9781316620083

© Cambridge University Press 1916

First published 1916
First paperback edition 2016

A catalogue record for this publication is available from the British Library

ISBN 978-1-316-62008-3 Paperback

PREFACE

THE present work is the result of long reflections, but was actually called forth by Professor Juvalta's *Old and New Problem of Morality*, to which my attention was drawn by Mr Benn's review in *Mind* (January, 1915). The instantaneous impression made by the review, in spite of the reviewer's disagreement with the author, was, "This is the doctrine of which I was in search." Though "awakened from dogmatic slumber" by Renouvier (*Mind* and the *Critique Philosophique*, 1887), I had for long continued the attempt to derive the ethical law of justice from "ends" or "goods." This is of course the tradition of English ethics; and my own resistance to Renouvier's Kantianism was only one expression of the effort of English thought to avoid the "*a priori*." The *a priori*, however, in some sense, cannot be avoided. English Experientialism, largely justified though it was and is, must inevitably be modified in the end by the Continental Rationalism that found its most powerful expression in Kant.

On this, I am glad to find myself in agreement with Mr Bertrand Russell, whose case is, I think, similar to my own. That is to say, he has been brought to this position, not by the desire to find support, denied by English philosophy in its unofficial tradition, for extra-philosophical convictions, but by the force of intellectual necessity. Still, having arrived at a modified view, we must "follow the argument"; and, if a metaphysical doctrine emerges that is more in harmony with the moral aspirations of mankind, we must not refuse to consider it out of a kind of willed austerity. There is, I think, something of this in Mr Russell. For my own part, whether on one side or the other, I decline to accept any limitations but those of necessity. As I refuse to decide for a doctrine simply on the ground that it is good for us to believe it, so also I refuse to bar out the consideration of it simply on the ground that we cannot arrive at scientific certainty.

The acceptance of an element of *a priori* law in ethics has at the present time a very distinct practical bearing. If by reflective thought, without reference to ends egoistic or altruistic, we recognise in ourselves and others rights which it is ethically wrong that any force should suppress, then, even in the hour of a defeat supposed final in the universe, the idea of right would still affirm itself: "Victrix causa deis placuit, sed victa Catoni." In the words with which Juvalta closes his treatise: *Liberum esse hominem est necesse; vivere non est necesse.* This once recognised, we have an ethical doctrine that enables us to judge of political systems. For the moralist, States no longer present themselves as mere competitive organisms the value of which is perhaps to be determined by their survival in evolution. It is not to be denied that the judgment of the moralist may help to determine which shall survive and which shall perish, or that the result of historical evolution may ultimately coincide with the moral judgment of mankind. This, however, does not affect the moral question itself. Even ultimately successful iniquity would none the less be iniquity. If we hold that wrong will not finally triumph, that belief springs from a metaphysical conviction subsequent to our ethical position, and on which this did not depend and can never come to depend for its ethical validity.

"The primary and fundamental values of every moral system," to adopt Mr Benn's statement of Professor Juvalta's general position, are "Liberty and Justice." These, I have always held, furnish the link between ethics and politics. The only change of attitude I have to indicate here is the definite recognition in them of an ethically *a priori* element. From this point of view, I am not in the least moved to scepticism by Mr Benn's objection that "there are great systems of morality in which neither liberty nor justice, as we understand them, find a place. They might be sought for in vain in a recent manifesto signed by the representatives of German art, intellect and religion[1]." The reply may very well be, in the words of Heraclitus, "One is ten thousand to me, if he be the best." Kant outweighs them all; and we know what his judgment would have been. The appeal is not to general consent, but to reflective thought. In the light of this, there is no reason why we should call such systems "systems of morality" at all. A code of conduct adapted to promote efficiently the organic life and expansion of an aggregate, but recognising no ultimate ground save a Collective Will, never seemed to me to

[1] After writing this Preface, I heard with regret of the death of Mr Benn (on the 16th of September, 1915). To avoid any misunderstanding, I must add that I do not suppose Mr Benn disagreed with me in personal opinion on the actual question: the difference that I take to be implied concerns the judgment we have the right to pronounce as moral philosophers.

deserve the name of morality in the proper sense. It might easily be the code of a band of robbers. And, as a matter of fact, a criminal State is not a new thing in history. Its punishment also will not be a new thing. Assyria at last became too intolerable for the ancient East, as the Kingdom of Prussia may have become too intolerable for the modern West.

Kant, as will be seen in Chapter VI of the present Essay, has by anticipation discussed the actual case, and has passed a somewhat lenient judgment. Briefly, it amounts to this, that the other nations are entitled to secure themselves henceforth by abolishing the institutions of the military monarchy, but not by destroying the offending State. Whatever may be thought of this judgment, it will not be denied that it is remote enough to be dispassionate.

T. W.

November 1915

CONTENTS

CHAPTER I

METAPHYSICAL PRELIMINARIES

"That the mind of man will ever once for all give up metaphysical inquiries is as little to be expected as that we shall sometime stop breathing altogether in order not to be always breathing impure air." So true is this assertion of Kant[1] that, although I regard the ethical thesis to be set forth as completely detachable from every metaphysical doctrine, I find it desirable to begin by a general statement of my metaphysical position in order to leave no ambiguity as to any lurking assumptions in the reasoning. For although ethics has to be constituted as an independent doctrine, there are certain relations of congruity between general positions regarding the foundations of ethics and of metaphysics. A modification in the traditionally empirical direction of English thought, bringing it nearer to philosophical rationalism, is likely to be simultaneous in all the philosophical sciences, and not limited to one. The modification of this kind which I agree with others in thinking necessary in metaphysics can be very briefly stated; and the statement of it will have the advantage of showing that the modification

[1] *Prolegomena zu einer jeden künftigen Metaphysik, die als Wissenschaft wird auftreten können*, Anhang.

in ethics is not an incongruous patch, but organically connected with a systematic readjustment. Further, at the end of the present essay, I shall have to point out that the ethical thesis suggests a certain metaphysical conclusion. For this reason, even if there were no other, a brief statement of metaphysical doctrine in so far as it is undetermined by ethics must come at the beginning. Thus it will be made clear exactly how the two philosophical doctrines are interrelated.

The preliminary statement of metaphysical positions can be limited to theory of knowledge. First, what is the meaning of the propositions we make about existences? Philosophers agree in recognising the existence of minds as apparent unities to which perceptions are referred, and of the external world as an apparent order scientifically calculable because it goes on in accordance with what is called the "uniformity of nature." But what is the method by which minds are to know about nature and about themselves? The antithetic views are those that have taken for their watchwords Reason and Experience. The philosophic Rationalist, if he is consistent, denies the name of science to the collections of facts and empirical generalisations which in the study of nature precede deductions made from principles. Of course experience is not on this view neglected; it admittedly furnishes the problems; and admittedly deductions from principles are shown to be wrong if the experience to which they refer does not confirm them. Still, reason with its first principles is predominant; and the sciences that have in them most of the matter of experience and least of the form of reason are in the lowest place. Rationalism in this sense, in spite of differences of relative stress in the schools of antiquity as in later schools, may be said to have predominated in the ancient classical conception of science. A change that can only be called revolutionary, both as regards the sciences of nature and man, was brought into the notion of the general method to be followed in seeking truth, by what has come to be known as the English school of philosophy. The line of thinkers of which the great names are Bacon, Hobbes, Locke, Berkeley, Hume, Mill and Spencer, placed a stress on experience that had never been systematically placed before[1]. The general position stated by Bacon was that in all our investigations we must above all take care to avoid importing the ideas of our own minds into nature. Only if we set ourselves to determine by all devices what happens in all circumstances may we hope at last to arrive at the true law of events and so to rule nature by obeying. A mark of "historical sense" in Bacon is that he detected a certain resemblance as regards method between the pre-Hellenic science of the ancient East, with its empiricism and its application to works of utility, and the aim that he was himself setting before the modern world[2]. The formal logic and deductive mathematics of the Greeks, which were the inspiration of their

[1] By no one has this been more decisively accepted than by Comte, who in theory of knowledge is to be classed wholly with the Experientialists. This in part explains his especially powerful influence in England.

[2] Cf. Comte, *Système de Politique Positive*, i. p. 429; "Quelque éminent que soit enfin devenu l'esprit positif, il ne doit jamais oublier qu'il émana partout de l'activité pratique, substituant graduellement l'étude des lois à celle des causes. Le principe universel de l'invariabilité des relations naturelles, sur lequel repose toute notre rationalité, est une acquisition essentiellement empirique." The principles themselves of mathematics Comte held to be empirical in basis.

1—2

philosophical rationalism, he was inclined to depreciate; disagreeing in the latter point with the Continental innovators who were his contemporaries. For, while Descartes was quite at one with Bacon in depreciating the logic of the mediaeval schools, with its basis in the Aristotelian formal logic, his hope was especially in the application of mathematical method. For the rest he was far from ignoring experience; and his practical aims had much in common with Bacon's, as may be seen by looking into his prefaces. He and the other leading Continental thinkers had also a perception that something new was coming from English thought. Yet the fundamental difference remains. For Descartes as for his great successors Spinoza and Leibniz, the test of truth is finally clearness in the principles and evidence in the reasonings. It was through the English mind that the distinctive spirit of modern experimental science first found expression in philosophy.

We are now, it seems to me, at the end of the period characterised by this division as regards method. It has several well-marked stages, of which the chief can easily be passed in review. For theory of knowledge, considered by itself and no longer as a direct means of approach to actual science, Locke's *Essay concerning Human Understanding* first definitely set the method of experiential, or "historical," inquiry into what we can know, against Descartes' statement of rational principles in the form of "innate ideas." The great importance of this was that it fixed for the future the English method of approach to philosophical problems through psychology. Locke, however, partly misapprehended Descartes' meaning; for Descartes did not suppose his "innate ideas" to be principles that were simply there once for all and could be discovered by itself in every human mind without trouble. It might sometimes appear as if he meant this; but he said himself on occasion that the innate ideas are only present potentially and need experience to develop them; and Leibniz, in his *Nouveaux Essais sur l'Entendement Humain*, expressly defended the Cartesian rationalism in that sense while making many concessions to Locke. The next important phase on the rationalist side was when Kant again restated the position, with new developments of the highest reach philosophically, in relation to the deduction of the ultimate consequences of experientialism by Hume on the basis of Locke and Locke's successor Berkeley. Ever since, the whole question of "theory of knowledge" has centred in Kant. Kant's general position being that certain rational principles, applied by the mind to experience, are necessary to constitute experience yet not derivable from it, whence they are called in his terminology *a priori* or "transcendental," these terms have since attached themselves to the rationalist view in philosophy; all the older forms of that view having yielded to Kantianism. For in fact Kant incorporated much from the thinkers who represented the opposite direction. His "transcendental" principles, he explained, though not derivable from experience, have no proper application beyond its limits. Thus the next great thinkers on the experientialist side, Comte and Mill, always spoke of him with respect, though their work was little affected by him; and Spencer, with hardly any direct knowledge of Kant, made spontaneous approaches to a theory of knowledge which included *a priori* forms. At the same time, Kant's disciples or successors both in France and in England succeeded in keeping the problems he had raised well before the minds of philosophers. The problems were never set at rest; and yet, somehow, we find that we are in a new phase. The oppositions are different. We are no longer distinctively Empiricists or Rationalists, but perhaps (for the present) Intellectualists or Volitionalists. And yet we are not very clear as to how it has come about, or where exactly we stand as regards the older controversies. For philosophy, which at least aspires to be self-conscious, this is not a satisfactory state of things. It seems desirable, if possible, that we should know our own minds. As I am not acquainted with any recent works that put the points more clearly than Mr Bertrand Russell's smaller and larger volumes, *The Problems of Philosophy* and *Our Knowledge of the External World as a Field for Scientific Method in Philosophy*, I shall try to define my own positions in relation to his.

First, I perfectly agree that "Logical knowledge is not derivable from experience alone, and the empiricist's philosophy can therefore not be accepted in its entirety[1]." "There are propositions known *a priori*, and among them are the propositions of logic and pure mathematics, as well as the fundamental propositions of ethics[2]." Soon, indeed, I come to a difference; and this is far-reaching, being a subtlety that seems to mark the beginning of divergence between the complete idealists and those who remain in some sense realists. To develop the difference,

---

[1] *Our Knowledge of the External World*, p. 37.
[2] *The Problems of Philosophy*, p. 125. I give the end of the sentence as well as the rest, though it is of course irrelevant at the present stage. This also I myself accept, as will be seen later.

however, will make clear the element of underlying agreement: for it does not affect the ratio between the factors of reason and experience in knowledge.

My most important difference on logic is that I regard the laws of formal logic as laws of thought, not of things. Here I follow Kant, who held them to be simply the principles of "analytic judgments"; that is, judgments that only make explicit what was before implicit, but do not add new knowledge, like the "synthetic judgments" (*a priori* or *a posteriori*) of mathematics and natural science. Yet I quite agree with Mr Russell when he points out that they are not psychological laws, that is, laws of our actual thinking. "What is important," Mr Russell says, "is not the fact that we think in accordance with these laws, but the fact that things behave in accordance with them, the fact that when we think in accordance with them we think *truly*[1]." "Thus the law of contradiction is about things, and not merely about thoughts; and although belief in the law of contradiction is a thought, the law of contradiction itself is not a thought, but a fact concerning the things in the world. If this, which we believe when we believe the law of contradiction, were not true of the things in the world, the fact that we were compelled to *think* it true would not save the law of contradiction from being false; and this shows that the law is not a law of *thought*[2]." To this I reply that certainly the law is not a law of thought merely as intellection (to use a term suggested by Croom Robertson). The establishment of the law belongs to metaphysics, not to psychology. It is a law of valid thought, not of

[1] *The Problems of Philosophy*, p. 113.
[2] *Ibid.*, p. 138.

thought as it is ascertained to take place. At the same time it is a law of analytic thought merely, and can reveal to us nothing that was not already contained in some "synthetic judgment," *a priori* or *a posteriori* as the case may be. If we have said that a thing momentarily existed, we must not deny that it momentarily existed; if we have said that it lasted such and such a time, similarly we must not deny this; but by the mere law of contradiction we cannot pass from the assertion of momentary existence to the denial that the existence was only for the moment. Yet, while it is not a law about things, it may be called a law of valid thought about things. What we need in order to make use of it is to furnish ourselves with some true general assertion or assertions of material import. Such assertions, I agree with Mr Russell, are to be found in the fundamental propositions of mathematics and in the law of causation. These are, in Kantian language, "synthetic," not merely "analytic."

Are they *a priori*, and, if so, in what sense? About the distinctive mathematical judgments, on which the existence of mathematics as a science depends, Kant's answer, I hold, is right: they are synthetic judgments *a priori*. Whatever may remain to be said about them psychologically is subordinate and does not affect the philosophical position, that their truth as laws is immediately evident in the construction itself by which the intellect brings them to light. The method of establishing their validity is not, as in the natural sciences, repetition of observations or experiments, but mental constructions within the universal forms of perception, viz., time and space. For their application to things, however, further general propositions are necessary. Of these the most typical is the law of causation.

On the ground of pure experience Hume seemed to have reduced the relation of cause and effect to an ultimately irrational expectation that the future will resemble the past. Hume himself of course believed in natural causation as firmly as any one; witness his classical statement of determinism alike for mind and things, and more especially his "Essay on Miracles." Kant therefore quite rightly treated his sceptical result as a question, not a solution. His answer in general terms is that anything we can call "nature" or "experience" would not be possible without a certain constitution of mind not derived from experience. Given experiential data, and sequences of events among them, we "make" a particular sequence, which presents itself at first as mere sequence, "necessary," by adding something from the mind. That is to say, we impose the relation of cause and effect on mere "subjective" data of sense; and thus for what would otherwise be no more than a play of dreaming phantasy we substitute a system that can be called in the proper sense nature as the object of science.

The unsatisfactory point in this answer was that it seemed to make the relation arbitrary in a way in which it obviously is not. We cannot help thinking of relations of cause and effect as "given" in the sense that the mind has to find them out and conform to them. Is this reconcilable with the validity of Kant's answer, that the relation of cause and effect is a "category" of the mind imposed on the sensible data? Difficult as the reconciliation may seem at first sight, I think it can be attained by a further evacuation of the *a priori* forms of Kant,—but an evacuation that is not destruction.

We must not suppose the mind equipped with a set of ready-made forms which it imposes on the flux of feeling. It is not true that we make a particular sequence, which is at first mere sequence, necessary by imposing a "category of the understanding," and thus constitute a particular relation of a cause to an effect. But also, it is not true that the order of perception simply as given imposes the relation of cause and effect on the mind. In rational science, the movement of thought is this. The mind, having formed an ideal of knowledge by exercise in logic and mathematics—which need not have gone very far—seeks to impose its own ideal of necessary connexion on that which it finds in perception. Already in perception certain uniformities have been established empirically which suggest the possibility of realising this ideal; but most perception goes on without any apparent stringency of connexion, as if things could simply come into and go out of existence, or as if, in Hume's phrase, anything could cause anything. To make a truly "objective" nature, as Kant said, the mind has to import something. What it does is to assert, and then to seek for, relations analogous to those of logical and mathematical necessity. For the logician, the "consequent" in a hypothetical argument necessarily follows from the "ground." Then in nature one event must follow from another with similar rigorous necessity. And in fact, not by applying ready-made forms that we have tabulated, but by persistently trying, with a generalised ideal of necessity in the mind, it is found that nature can more and more be interpreted as a system of necessary relations. From mere subjective flux of perception, it becomes "experience" in Kant's sense. We at length find laws that are not mere rules, but theorems admitting of no exception, as if nature were logic and mathematics realised, to be the only kind of laws according to which experience can be coherently thought.

But is not the test, it may be said from the experientialist side, simply verification by perception? We begin with observation, we proceed by thought and experiment, and finally we appeal to what we find actually goes on. The reply is that this is true in all particular cases; but that if we take into our view the whole activity of science at any time, the verification is never complete; and yet we know that we shall always hold to our ideal of necessary connexion against any appearance of uncertainty or caprice. This is the inexpugnable element of philosophical rationalism involved in the scientific view of nature. However evacuated the element of the *a priori* becomes, it cannot be effaced.

The complementary truth enforced by experientialism is that only on the condition of attending to things and events and adapting its behaviour to them in the minutest detail, suppressing every disposition to dictate what the particular connexions must be, can the mind ever come to understand them.

But what ultimately are these things and events in nature? Here the answers of philosophers seem to have depended little on the degree in which their theory of knowledge was experiential or rationalist. Kant's general answer did not differ from that of the English; that the sciences of nature deal with phenomena, that is to say, appearances for minds. Yet, though none but this "idealist" view was consistent with his positions, he took fright at the term when it was applied to him, thinking he was being accused of the absurdities popularly attributed to Berkeley. Of Berkeley it is clear from his references that he had no knowledge whatever; and of Hume, while he knew and had carefully studied the *Inquiry* and the *Dialogues concerning Natural Religion*, it is evident that he had not read the more radically sceptical *Treatise of Human Nature*. Thus the *Critique of Pure Reason* did not start at all points from the most advanced critical positions already attained; and in the second edition, through fear of having his "Transcendental idealism" classed with the idealism of Berkeley, he introduced new complication and obscurity into a work already sufficiently difficult; bringing back apparently the confused notion of a material object that is ultimately non-phenomenal. In reality this, as a clear-headed successor like Schopenhauer saw, is as inconsistent with the Kantian criticism of knowledge as Berkeley had already shown it to be with the subjectively critical point of view common to Descartes and Locke.

When I speak of the confused notion of a non-phenomenal material object, I do not mean the "thing-in-itself" or "things-in-themselves." This, whether we continue to use the term or not, was quite soundly distinguished from phenomena. It meant properly metaphysical reality, of which the phenomena are the manifestation. Kant's expressions about the thing-in-itself are not entirely consistent; but the view to which he points most distinctly is that reality is a timeless system of ideas, which might be known, if a speculative metaphysic were possible, under the form of a Platonic

Intelligible World, but is actually most comprehensible as a system of ethical and aesthetic norms. For Hegel, reality was Thought, knowable in the actual world and manifested above all in history. For Schopenhauer it was Will, temporarily individualised in conscious beings. For Berkeley it was a system of spirits communicating by ideas (which are groupings of sense-elements), held in unity by a supreme personal spirit, which determines the sequence of ideas so that communication is possible in a common world of which, and of its parts, the being is to be perceived (*esse* is *percipi*). For Hume, if he had put his result in a dogmatic form, it would have been particular impressions (mental states) composing a flux in which individual personalities are temporary appearances of unification. All these ontological views, clearly, are consistent with idealism in the phenomenist sense; which of course does not in the least deny that what we call the external world indicates a reality, but denies that it is itself, in its appearance as objects and events in space and time, the reality from which minds can be explained. On this side of the doctrine, no one has ever refuted Berkeley.

The Berkeleyan idealism illustrates an interesting remark of Mr Russell, that the most hopeful thing for progress in any philosophical system is the element inexplicable on its own principles. Idealism of rationalist type, in the schools of antiquity descended from Plato, had shown quite effectively that mental processes cannot be explained from material processes in the organism. The phenomenist view of material things had also been attained as a doctrine. Berkeley, however, discovered, from the experientialist position of a disciple of Locke, a much more generally apprehensible way of proving the truth of the doctrine, now again emerging in modern philosophy. He proved it by means of the "surd" in ancient and modern materialism. According to Democritus, the reality is that which we know by touch. The atom, which ultimately resists effort, is "being"; void, which does not resist, but lets the atoms go through it, is a kind of real "not-being." Qualities such as sound, colour, and so forth, exist only "by convention"; that is, we talk about them as if they were really in things, but they are not. Modern physicists, when the time was ripe for the scientific application of atomism, carried forward this Democritean view. The ultimate realities, in their conception of the world, were resistant and extended particles like the atoms of Democritus. By the real motions of these real particles certain ideas of qualities—sound, colour, heat, now called "secondary qualities" as distinguished from the primary qualities of resistance and extension—are raised in us. These exist only in us, not in things, the reality of which is simply to be groups of variously agitated particles. Thus the "surd" remained; for clearly no explanation had been given of the "secondary qualities." You do not expel sensations from the world by calling them "conventional" or saying they only exist in us. Berkeley, in his fresh polemic against materialism, turned the accepted doctrines of the physicists against themselves; showed that the sensations on the ground of which we affirm the primary qualities are just as much in our minds as the others; that all alike, indeed, are as much "in us" as those typical examples of pure "subjectivity," pleasure and pain; finally, that of material substance, in distinction from groupings of perceptions, we neither know nor can conceive or imagine anything. This does not mean that the world with the things in it is unreal: on the contrary, all alike in the world is real, in the only sense in which it can be, as a constant order in our perceptions.

From this constant order we are entitled rationally to infer the existence of minds other than our own; simply because we perceive groupings of phenomena resembling our own organism, with which particular group of phenomena our own consciousness is associated in a peculiar way. Thus the common objection is met that the Berkeleyan idealism leads to "solipsism"; that is, to the assertion by an individual mind that it is the only real existence, other persons having no existence beyond their appearances. It is rationally met, that is to say; for I do not suppose that we actually come to believe in the existence of other persons by any such inference. The question for the philosopher, however, is, what we are entitled to believe, not, how we come to believe it. We believe many things on instinct to which the test of science or philosophy is applied with varying results. The Berkeleyan idealist finds that the analogical argument to other persons is both sound in itself and leads to an intelligible conclusion; whereas the notion of material substance, if analysed, leaves no residue that is non-phenomenal. Here, we may say, there is left only a confused notion vaguely pointing to metaphysics[1], but incapable of any properly scientific

[1] This is slightly to supplement Berkeley, who, at least in his first phase, did not concede so much as this. Kant, on the other hand, did not become quite clear of supposing that this notion can be something for science; which, on that view, would have an "object" that is neither pure phenomenon nor "thing-in-itself."

statement; for science has to do only with phenomena.

I do not know whether Mr Russell will find that this
meets his objections to idealism; but he has some
positive arguments for realism not yet touched upon.
With the portion of these that concerns the mathematical
infinite I shall try to deal. If this is knowable as a
"thing," and not merely as an "idea," then idealism as
I understand it must be abandoned. Now my knowledge
of mathematics is undoubtedly very small in comparison
with Mr Russell's; but the question of philosophical
principle seems to me to come near the beginning and
to concern the elements of the subject; and so I venture
to discuss it. I find no mystery in Mr Russell's ex-
positions, such as Berkeley found in those of contemporary
"analysts." They are to me quite intelligible, but all
quite explicable on the principles of idealism without
supposing infinite numbers to be real collections. The
true mode of explaining the infinite in mathematics
I seem to myself to have found in De Morgan and
Renouvier, one a philosophical mathematician, the other
a philosopher with a considerable knowledge of mathematics. What I have learnt from them I shall now try
to apply to infinite numbers. I take it to be merely
historical accident that the thinkers competent by special
knowledge to expound the more recent developments
in pure mathematics are realists. Their special knowledge has enabled them to display a subtlety in defending
their realism which, it seems to me, is unnecessary for
the defence of idealism. The "short way" that I propose
from the idealist point of view is this. There is no need
to contest what is said about the orders of infinite

numbers, and their relations to one another of greater
and less, paradoxical as these are. The "number of all
finite numbers," for example, is greater than the "number
of all finite squares"; and yet both are infinite, for
neither can be counted[1]. Since they cannot be thought
as results of counting, they are unthinkable as actual
collections; but the difficulty disappears if we regard
"infinite numbers" as names for certain processes in
mind that can be carried on indefinitely with application
to (phenomenal) objects, according to a certain law of
counting, different in different cases. We can make as
many terms as we like, and can apply them to objects
or parts of objects, but there is not an actually existent
infinite series of terms. The infinite series of fractions
less than 1[2] is really what Renouvier called an "indefinite
possibility" of dividing. We can make as many as we
like, and can go on applying them without limit to a
"continuous" magnitude, but there is not an infinite
series of actually existent fractions. To speak as if there
were is scientific shorthand for describing a continuous
quantity. So I can attach a meaning to calling the
number of all finite numbers and the number of all finite

[1] *Our Knowledge of the External World*, pp. 194–195 (comment on
a passage from Galileo's *Mathematical Discourses*). "It is actually the
case that the number of square (finite) numbers is the same as the
number of (finite) numbers....But although the infinite numbers which
Galileo discusses are equal, Cantor has shown that what Simplicius
[a personage in the Dialogue] could not conceive is true, namely, that
there are an infinite number of different infinite numbers, and that the
conception of *greater* and *less* can be perfectly well applied to them.
The whole of Simplicius's difficulty comes, as is evident, from his belief
that, if *greater* and *less* can be applied, a part of an infinite collection
must have fewer terms than the whole; and when this is denied, all
contradictions disappear."

[2] *Ibid.*, pp. 178–179.

squares equally infinite numbers though the first is greater than the second, only if this is taken as scientific shorthand (not to say "useful nonsense"). When they are brought under the conditions of thought, I find no puzzle. The infinity of both series alike means that you can carry both beyond any assignable number of terms. That the first is greater than the second means that, wherever you stop, the whole is greater than its part. If you do not stop, there is no whole.

Thus, so far as I can see, there is nothing in the mathematical theory of the infinite which, when clearly conceived, requires us to suppose collections of real things that do not comply with the conditions of phenomenal presentation. Whether in its *a priori* or *a posteriori* elements, science is alike phenomenal. On this side the admission of a certain element of metaphysical Rationalism makes no difference to English Idealism as theory of knowledge. It is true that pure phenomenism is insufficient for philosophy; that we need a theory of being as well as of appearance; but, as has been briefly indicated, there are many possible idealistic ontologies. This is all that was necessary in an introduction to an essay of which the direct object is not metaphysical. Indeed I must next point out that the principles of ethics not only do not depend on any of the possible ontological doctrines, but do not even depend on the generalised theory of knowledge to which I have almost exclusively limited myself.

CHAPTER II

SEPARATION OF ETHICS FROM METAPHYSICS

The classical statement of the separation of ethics from metaphysics is that of Hume's *Treatise*[1], where he objects to systems of morality in general that they proceed as if *ought* or *ought not* can follow immediately, without the introduction of any new principle, from *is* or *is not*. This applies historically both to systems called naturalistic and to those called rationalistic; though, as Professor Carveth Read has observed[2], not to all. Of those to which it does not apply, the systems that may be most conveniently singled out are those of Aristotle and Kant; for, on the next question of general principle to be discussed, these are antithetic. Both are very complex and in their own manner include everything; but Aristotle's system is directed by the idea of moral end, Kant's by that of moral law. Neither, of course, is without metaphysical points of contact, but essentially they are both free from the fallacy of trying to deduce what is to be done by man from the mere nature of some reality. Aristotle holds that in attaining the highest good, which is contemplative thought, man is so far imitating the life of

[1] Book III, Part i, sect. 1.
[2] *Natural and Social Morals*, p. 6.

2—2

God; but he would still regard thought as man's highest good even if it were simply a good for man, and not (as he holds that it is) realised perpetually in Mind that thinks only itself. Kant, in the *Practical Reason*, contends for an affirmation that the universe is so ruled as to join happiness to man's observance of the moral law; but he holds that law to be completely obligatory for man whatever the constitution of the universe may be. This is to be clear of the fallacy pointed out by Hume, as neither Platonism nor Stoicism is clear of it. No doubt in both these cases the ethical teaching of the school admits of a statement to which logical objection could not be taken; but, in so far as it is professedly deduced from the theoretical doctrine, the logical objection is fatal. To determine the order of goods from the scale of beings according to the degree in which these are "real" is a most typical expression of the "metaphysical fallacy"; as the precept to "live according to nature" is a direct expression of the "naturalistic fallacy," which is merely another form of the first.

The writer who has tracked down these fallacies most effectively is Mr G. E. Moore in *Principia Ethica*. I do not propose to go over the ground again, but will briefly note on my own account that any speculative conclusions arrived at or suggested as possible in the preceding chapter do nothing at all to give us a starting-point in ethics. That reality is to be expressed in terms of mind tells us nothing in relation to conduct that is not already obvious. For it is obvious that the existence of ethics depends on the existence of minds in some sense; but whether these are temporary or permanent existences, existences not referable to anything non-mental as their cause or simply determinations (if this were intelligible) of material things, makes no difference to the ethical question, how shall minds regulate their conduct in so far as it is in their power to regulate it. Science and metaphysics can tell us, or assume to tell us, much about our power and its limits and about the nature of the things among which we are placed; but the question for ethics concerns our choice when there is a choice, and this supposes that actually something is at present undetermined, that is, not yet realised, not yet part of anything that is there whether we will it or not. In asserting this "apparent freedom of choice," which is all that is required, we are not asserting anything metaphysical, but a mere datum like the existence of our thoughts and feelings and of certain objects that may or may not be more than groupings of phenomena. Thus, for the purpose of ethical inquiry, we may place ourselves in the beginning simply at the common-sense point of view, assuming nothing but minds (temporary or permanent) among objects (temporary or permanent) able to act (whatever this may ultimately mean) upon objects and, through objects, upon each other. The more we know about fact or reality, whether scientifically or metaphysically, the more conditions of choice there will be; but the essence of the choice must always depend on what we think we ought to do so far as the fact is not already determined apart from us; for if it is so determined we have no choice. Even then, to acquiesce in not having a choice is a kind of action of our own, to which the term *ought* or *ought not* may be applicable. And *ought* or *ought not*, here too, is not deducible from the bare fact.

Perhaps an even more distinctive part of Mr Moore's work than his refutation of the naturalistic and metaphysical fallacies is his refutation of Hedonism as usually understood. Here he depends much for starting-points on the *Philebus* of Plato, to which it will always be necessary to go back when any subtlety is aimed at in the discussion of pleasure in its relation to ends considered as desirable. That pleasure is actually aimed at, Mr Moore elaborately shows on the model of his preceding discussions, does not prove that it ought to be aimed at. What he himself is in search of is a scale of goods or values arranged, we might put it, in the order of their objective preferableness. Of course all moral philosophers aim at objectivity in the sense of universality. The naturalistic and metaphysical fallacies arose from the search for something general to place above the mere temporary choice of the will. For some who had seen through these, hedonism seemed to have fixed on something of the kind, because pleasure and absence of pain were apparently identical with universally preferable feeling. But is the preferableness of a total state identical with its preferableness when compared with other states simply as regards the quantity of pleasure[1] it includes? Plato, merely by submitting the question in the concrete to intuitive judgment, showed that it is not. He made it perfectly clear on the one side that, ready as we may be to allow that knowledge is a good, we should not desire a perpetual state of the completest and most conscious knowledge (if it could exist) without a trace of pleasurable

---

[1] This is put for simplicity. Mr Moore has gone through all the complexities that come into view when pleasure and pain are considered as present or absent or in various degrees coexistent.

feeling. On the other side, we should not desire the perpetuity of a state in which we were steeped in pleasure without consciousness of any intellectual relation, a state in which we knew nothing for ever but were all feeling, like a beatified oyster. Thus the problem of the desirable life has to be solved by determining a certain mixture in which both knowledge and pleasure shall have their part. Starting thence, Mr Moore has followed up the problem with extreme subtlety, and with results which seem to me on the whole sound. In the study of his results I have myself arrived at an additional hedonic paradox.

The element of truth in hedonism, I hold, as I have consistently held, is that unless there goes with it some subjective accompaniment of feeling which is regarded as preferable to other feelings, no state or process can be itself an object of preference[1]. It is understood of course that we are speaking of preference by self-conscious or reflective thought. Mr Moore, a little more doubtfully, decides in the same sense; but the contention that interests him most is that "intrinsic value" is not proportional to pleasure. In a different way I have allowed this by definitely rejecting Bentham's notion of happiness as consisting of an algebraical sum of pleasures and pains; pleasures counting as positive and pains as negative quantities. Happiness, I argued, is a total state of the personality not even in theory to be estimated by any calculus, because it is not definable in hedonic terms through and through[2]. Mr Moore, when that was written,

---

[1] I still adhere to the expression of this in a review of Professor Sorley's *Ethics of Naturalism* (1st ed.), *Mind*, O.S. xi. 265 (April, 1886).
[2] *The Liberal State* (1907), p. 25.

had already worked out the theory of hedonism and the objections to it with far more exactitude. His general position is finally that we can add to the intrinsic value (the preferableness) of a total state by adding something that is not pleasure; consequently, pleasure will not serve by itself to test the ends of action. Moreover, total value may be greatly increased by adding something which by itself has little or no value, or even negative value. The subject of intrinsic value will recur later: in the meantime I state my own paradox, which I have not found anticipated either in *Principia Ethica* or in the smaller *Ethics*[1].

Let us suppose a universe without either pleasure or pain: such a universe would be made better by introducing some pain and no positive pleasure. For in the former universe there could be no preferred subjective state and therefore no end and no good; while in the latter tranquillity would be a desired state, an end and a good. This is in fact the world as Plato in one of his hedonic speculations supposed it to be, and as it was afterwards supposed to be by Epicurus; what we call pleasures being held to consist only in release from pain. Such a world, I contend, if there are means of overcoming the pain and attaining intervals of the desired tranquillity, is better than that for which we have supposed it substituted.

I do not myself regard this as the actual constitution of our world, but recognise the existence of positive pleasures. These are a part of the ends of action, and the consideration of them helps us to classify some goods; though the "hedonical calculus" certainly will not enable

[1] A passage in *Ethics*, p. 244, is on the verge of it.

us to fix our larger preferences. But if out of these
preferences we are to construct an ethical doctrine, there
must necessarily be some attempt to reach the kind of
agreement that the hedonists prematurely thought to
be attained or attainable. Such an attempt, however
often it may fail, does not seem in itself chimerical.
Preferences have changed historically, partly through
argument. Ideal goods have become more distinctly
conceived; and there is an art of persuasion by which
they may be brought under common points of view that
will determine their rank in opinion. There is also some
spontaneous convergence. Mr Moore's estimate of the
things that have most intrinsic value differs little from
Comte's final estimate, and seems to have been arrived
at independently. Among intrinsic goods, he puts in the
highest place aesthetic enjoyments and personal affections,
with knowledge in the third place and subordinated to
the first. Professor Carveth Read, following Aristotle
and Spinoza in making philosophy the highest good,
takes a view less unlike the preceding than might at
first appear; for philosophy, thus conceived, is of course
not any kind of mere special knowledge, but includes as
elements beauty and "intellectual love." And the highest
good does not mean the sole and exclusive good.

But in the end, whatever further agreement may be
reached through discussion and arts of persuasion, have
we arrived at anything that can be called ethics proper?
Or are we still, as Mr Moore implies in the claim he makes
for his *Principia Ethica*, only at the stage of prolegomena?
In my opinion, we are only at that stage. The most
distinctive part of ethics has not yet come into view.

CHAPTER III

END AND LAW IN ETHICS

So far, it has been assumed that the end of action is
a good to be pursued; and this in general terms is incontestable. Without some good in view as a conscious
end, there would be no rational as distinguished from
instinctive action. Ethics is of course concerned properly
with rational action; that is, with conduct directed by
some general conception to which it is held that particular
actions ought to conform. But what is the meaning of
this word *ought*? Does it merely mean that, given a
certain end, the way of reaching it pointed out by the
law of causation must be adopted if we do not wish to
miss it? Or does the word apply also to the end; so
that it can be said we ought to choose such and such
a good? And if we choose the wrong end or take the
wrong way to the right end, what is to be said? Are
we simply unwise, either through want of sufficient
knowledge or of consistency with ourselves, or through
not having been rightly persuaded about the value of one
good in distinction from another? Or is there the
possibility that we are wrong in a sense that does not
mean exactly the same as unwise?

Some would say that there is nothing in the case but

unwisdom, perhaps in extreme cases a mental infirmity analogous to disease. The function of the moral philosopher is to make the relative value of goods an object of clear knowledge. The educator and the practical moralist, trained in the philosophical schools, must apply arts of persuasion in order to impress the true system on the general mind. In extreme cases of missing the good, the State may apply remedies in the form of penalties; partly for the sake of others, because they are liable to suffer injury, and penalties inflicted deter those who might imitate the actions of the offender; and partly in order to cure the offender himself, whose welfare is for its own sake an object of interest to other members of the community.

But already in this view we find implicitly a principle more expressly formulated by moralists who find the idea not simply of unwisdom but of moral wrong in a more distinctive sense in certain modes of pursuing ends. In the view just stated, it is to be observed that the moralist, theoretical or practical, the educator, and the legislator, are all supposed to be actuated by motives of general benevolence. Now many of the moralists known as Utilitarians find the idea of rightdoing in action according to the principle of general benevolence or "altruism," that is, in seeking the good of others or of all, and the idea of wrongdoing in aiming exclusively at one's own good to the disadvantage of others or in indifference to them.

This at first sight comes nearer to the notion conveyed by Ethics. Morality in the popular view is not identified with prudence or with intellectual consistency. In the system that attempts this identification, it would seem to an outsider that the moral interests of life are represented more especially by the philosophers, educators and legislators. And a modern utilitarian might very plausibly argue that that is because the principle of general benevolence is represented most in them. They aim at the good of all spontaneously. The rest of the community they treat as their charges, to be disciplined into right for their own good by having the appropriate trains of associated ideas set going in their minds. For the existence of morality, then, we must suppose spontaneous altruism somewhere. This is the true spring of it all.

When we come to the application, however, difficulties soon arise. There seems to be a more definite and stringent meaning of right and wrong than has hitherto come into view. This meaning does not depend simply on the contrast between egoism and altruism. It may be made to appear as if it did by using the "question-begging epithets," as Bentham might have called them, of "selfish" and "unselfish," and then asserting that selfishness is always wrong and unselfishness always right. As a matter of fact, there is every kind of complication. Self-assertion may be in some circumstances a right and a duty; self-sacrifice may be wrong. If there are "intrinsic values," these must be known to be such for ourselves before we can seek them for others; so that egoism cannot even in the ideal be extruded from human life. And, when we have our scheme of values, are we to sacrifice for ourselves a value that we regard as elevated in order to procure for others something we regard as contemptible? Nothing could be more unselfish, but many moralists would think it wrong. Let us suppose

that a few persons in a community desire freedom while
the majority would be more comfortable in slavery and
know that they would be. The few, on the other hand,
who desire freedom, know that they are at least strong
enough, if they choose, to make acquiescence too un-
comfortable for the rest. Much misery, however, will
be caused in the struggle. Shall they "unselfishly"
submit in order to avoid this and to give the majority
the kind of happiness they desire and can understand?
Milton, at least, who was a moralist, would have despised
the decision in such a case to comply with the desires of
those who love more "bondage with ease than strenuous
liberty."

This illustration brings into view the ethical doctrine
which in modern times has been set against all the forms
of that which has been hitherto considered. What we
have to determine primarily, it is said, is not the good
that is to be the end of action, whether it is a good for
one or for all, whether it is to be pursued selfishly or
unselfishly, but the moral law to which actions ought to
conform. This moral law is not a deduction from any
end, but is valid simply as law. Its form is that of
reciprocal relations of right and duty. The general
expression for it is justice, to which actions prompted by
egoistic and altruistic motives are alike under the obligation
of submitting. This obligation is not imposed by any
external command, whether of a human or superhuman
legislator, but by the rational will of the individual
person, who imposes the law upon himself. The person
is "autonomous." At the same time the legislation is
universal, being applicable to all rational beings alike
under the same conditions. And this stringent obligation,

some have contended, is precisely that which protects human liberty from possible suppression by the benevolent utilitarianism which, under sanctions of persuasion or of force, would seek to promote good or happiness directly by authoritative systems of educative and of political institutions.

A utilitarian who values liberty might reply: I accept precisely what you call the law of justice, but as a means to the kind of community—a community of freemen—which to me is the end. This reply, however, when closely considered, seems to be political rather than properly ethical. No doubt if a community prefers or can be persuaded to prefer liberty, it will, if it desires to survive, adopt the means to that end. But what is there, ethically, to distinguish the taste of a number of persons who prefer liberty from the taste of a number of other persons who prefer despotism? Only a doctrine like that of the moral law regarded as supreme over all ends, its adherents finally insist, can determine the question of right.

And the appeal of the doctrine is two-sided. If it is held to be the only firm ground of political liberty, a powerful appeal is also made to the conservative mind when the idea of supreme moral law is found to go back to the hoariest antiquity. The unwritten and eternal laws associated with divinity in the famous passages of Sophocles—the speech of Antigone to Creon[1] and the chorus in the *Oedipus Tyrannus*[2]—are not appealed to as new but as immemorial. In Aeschylus, justice is the appanage of the elder gods or of impersonal Fate, whose

---

[1] *Ant.* 450–470.   [2] *Oed. T.* 863–871.

inviolable Right will bring the new Powers that have set themselves against it to their doom.

Yet, old as is this generalised assertion of moral law, it was never, in the explicit systems of Greek philosophy, made ostensibly the directing principle. This was always the idea of end, in subordination to which the moral virtues were classified as aptitudes for attaining it. Justice, however, where if anywhere the idea of law prevails, was always regarded as the chief social virtue; and Aristotle, it has been noticed, does not derive it immediately from the end, but from quasi-mathematical notions. In modern times, on the other hand, while the same precedence has not always been accorded to justice, the idea of moral law has at length come to be formulated in the way that we have seen. The first to receive poetic it has been the last to receive scientific expression.

But is there not, some may ask, a universally valid norm in the idea of end or good? Mr Moore proposes a way that seems in theory to get rid not only of all difficulties about egoism and altruism, but of all conflict between moral law and end, by declaring the right action to be always that of which in the long run the consequences are the greatest total good in the universe. As good is the objectively preferable, the greatest total of good in the universe is theoretically capable of being known. And, as I must treat myself impartially simply as one element in the total, there can never be any question whether I ought to be egoistic or altruistic: my duty to myself and others is simply the distribution that will give the greatest total good. My right, clearly, is coextensive with my duty. I ought to have precisely the share of good that it is my duty to assign to myself.

Against this, there are two arguments. First, we are not omniscient beings, as we should have to be to know the total consequences of an action. These are knowable only in the sense that knowledge of them by omniscience is conceivable. From this it follows that we can never know what is right. But in fact we know that in most cases we do know what is right. Therefore, to know what is right it is not necessary to know the total consequences of an action. Secondly, suppose a being who knows all and determines what shall be. Then, from the point of view of the ethics of law, since the universe includes persons, its total good cannot be determined apart from ultimately just relations among persons. The law therefore even in the mind of omniscience is not wholly derivative from an end that does not include it. This reply is conclusive at the present stage, because to reject a type of ethics not yet examined would be to beg the question.

The positive argument for holding moral law rather than end or good to be the most distinctive thing in ethics is a stringency in certain ethical judgments that never seems derivable even from our own most decisive estimates of goods. At least I have tried and failed to derive it in my own case. Though I have no doubt that justice is connected as a means with liberty as an end in politics, I have not found that derivation ethically sufficient for the establishment of the principles of justice. And when we define good by a less abstract term than the political end, its insufficiency to support properly ethical judgments becomes more obvious.

Let us try to find a substitute in Comte's formulation of "altruism" as the characteristically ethical attitude.

For if there is any hope of general agreement, it might seem to be here. Devotion to Humanity, in the whole complex of its interests, is to be supreme; but under it various ideal directions are allowed. Art or knowledge, for example, may rightly be pursued as ideal ends. Those who select these ends, Comte recognises, must have an impassioned interest in them, not simply determined by relation to the ethical direction of life. No artist or man of science could more emphatically declare that intellectual or artistic work done from a sense of duty without enjoyment in the exercise of the special faculty would be valueless. But, this granted, he also declares that the aim of serving Humanity must be supreme. Specialism undirected by some general idea, or the cultivation of technical accomplishment out of relation to any wide view of nature or human life, are to be conscientiously repressed by the student or artist who feels a temptation to them; and, if they are not thus repressed, public opinion ought to disapprove of them as immoral deviations. Now, so far as I myself am concerned, I am quite willing to comply with that condition, and to test my pursuits or have them tested in relation to general interests of Humanity. In the study of the history of philosophy, for example, I indulge no purely antiquarian impulse; if I study a special period, it is for the sake of getting a grasp of the historical movement as a whole with a bearing on the present. Thus, I have no personal interest in maintaining that the moral criterion is not applicable in the way that Comte holds; but actually I do not find it applicable in that way. If any one has more decidedly the impulses of a specialist, I think he has a right to follow them. Minute curiosity, or the attraction of some special kind of beauty, without any obvious human interest, may be the motives under which he can best work; and it is really a question of right. A case exactly to the purpose is that of Roger Bacon. It is quite possible that, from any social point of view, what was needed in the thirteenth century was not the direction of thought to physical science. None the less, I hold that the restriction of his scientific researches by authority was absolutely a wrong. What his own motives were is quite irrelevant to the question of right. He may have been seeking his highest good in the satisfaction of curiosity. He may, like Francis Bacon afterwards, have had a prevision of the social services to be rendered by science in a future age. If he had this prevision, it may have been accompanied by philanthropic emotion or by pure indifference. In any case, his right was not ethically suppressible by his Society's as opposed to his own choice of good. When Comte speaks of duties as alone existent without rights, he uses a term to which he is not entitled. If other persons have no rights, or if Humanity has no rights, how can there be a duty to serve them? In actual fact, the violation of justice (to which Comte personally was very sensitive) makes a totally different impression from anything we can derive ethically from our own or any one's choice of good. The choice of good may be largely an affair of rational preference; we may think that persons who choose differently fail in rationality; but, till the question of justice comes in, there does not seem to be that which characterises strictly moral approval or disapproval. This is really unique; and it is here, I hold, that the *a priori* element in ethics is inexpugnable.

On the other hand, Utilitarian thinkers are irrefutable when they insist on the emptiness of all efforts to deduce actual human conduct from abstract rights and duties. It is quite true that, to get anything out of their formulae, the pure Rationalists have to introduce utilitarian considerations (references to ends or goods) surreptitiously. What Utilitarians cannot get out of their ends is stringent obligation.   What Rationalists cannot get out of their forms or laws is any actual end to be pursued.   Now here I think comes in the reconciliation.   Just because the ends are not in themselves obligatory, while yet all the content of human life depends on them, there is room for the selection of different ends.   But, while these are not pointed out by the moral law, the moral law assigns limiting conditions of their pursuit.   It is at certain critical points, where these conditions are definitely in question, that strictly moral choice occurs.   To make the right or wrong choice in these critical cases is to succeed or fail in the observance of justice or the moral law. Thus there is no specially "moral life"; but morality in the distinctive sense is of universal obligation.   What is sometimes thought to be the ideally moral life, namely, the life of philanthropy or of extended altruism, is one ideal direction not necessarily more moral than any other. Psychologically it may be directed by love in the most enlarged sense; but love as a psychological principle is not a criterion, but is simply the natural spring of all social action.   This is quite clearly so if we include "self-love," and self-love can reasonably be included according to Comte's sociological view; for, man being fundamentally social, his egoism can never be that of an isolated animal being; or at least this limit is reached only in the lower order of criminals, who, as Comte says, are less organic parts of Humanity than the domestic animals. It has often been noted what a strong social element there is even in the most egoistic ambitions; so that the egoist of really high intellect usually becomes, whether that is his direct aim or not, in some way greatly serviceable to human life.

It appears then on the whole clear that various types may have the right to choose different kinds of good and to pursue them in their difference, and that all may be equally moral in doing this. No one, however, can say that he has the *right* to disregard justice. This proposition is not merely verbal; for, as will be seen, justice is not one end among others, to be taken or left, but assigns the conditions under which all ends are to be pursued. Right and wrong, in the strict and not merely vague sense, are predicates of relations among persons, and not of the total consequences of an action. In human action, it is possible to know right and wrong, but impossible to know what action will have the best possible consequences. Still, the intelligence that applies the moral law, as well as the intelligence that calculates consequences, is fallible; so that cases of doubt are unavoidable. The *a priori* moralists have never been able to avoid them any more than the Utilitarians. Perhaps it is the *a priori* elements in moral systems that have been the most fertile in casuistry. Casuistry cannot be eluded. In the mode of reconciliation put forward, indeed, both consequences and *a priori* principles are relevant in all actual decisions as to what we shall do. The position, however, seems to me to be simplified rather than complicated by this admission; because it leaves relatively few cases distinctively cases of moral

END AND LAW IN ETHICS

conscience. For, if our general mode of life is compatible with the rule of right, clearly the larger part of what we have to consider depends on consequences, and the means to learning these is knowledge and practice in our own mode of life: we have not to be considering at every moment the bearings of our ethical code. Stringency of the doctrine in one aspect can thus coexist with the highest degree of spontaneity on the part of the individual in choosing and following the good.

The generalised doctrine of right or justice I propose to call distinctively Abstract Ethics. The pursuit of good in its detail may be called the Art of Life, but in reality this consists of many arts, instinctive, empirical, or deduced from some branch or branches of science as the case may be. Concrete or Applied Ethics is concerned with the pursuit of good when it comes into contact with the principles of Abstract Ethics. By this division the defects both of the purely *a priori* and the purely *a posteriori* systems are avoided. The error of both, where they were in error, was in exaggerating the function of the moral philosopher. The ideal of moral philosophy was supposed to be the furnishing of a code for daily practice through the whole of life. But only a very morbid life can ever be a perpetual series of cases of conscience. The position of abstract ethics as a science resembles most that of logic. Thought does not go on, in the logician any more than in any one else, as an application of the laws of logic; but those laws can be applied if necessary as its test. So also action does not go on in the ethical philosopher any more than in any one else by way of regular deduction from moral principles, but the moral law can be applied as its test in case of doubt; or if action is challenged from outside as wrong and not merely as unwise, its defence must be in terms of the moral law. "I did it for the best" may be accepted as an excuse when ends are in question. When an infringement of the law of justice is in question, it is not held to be an adequate reply.

Abstract Ethics is not a thing that remains to be constructed. What I propose to do next is to show where it is to be found. Then I shall proceed to develop the present distinctions in more detail.

CHAPTER IV

THE HISTORY OF ABSTRACT ETHICS

The foundation of abstract ethics dates from the seventeenth century. Though, as actual precepts, all the ideas that constitute it are to be met with in antiquity, and though a doctrine like Stoicism could now find the fittest expression in its terms, yet all the ancient systems may be called relatively concrete. So also may most of the ethical systems of modern times; for it is only by degrees that the difference in point of view has become clear; and it cannot even be said that there has been perfectly steady progress to its recognition. Indeed the movement in the nineteenth century rather tended to the view that abstract ethical discussion of rights and of justice could be nothing but an affair of more or less convenient, but sometimes dangerously misleading, fictions. We were concerned with the ends and the real conditions of conduct, not with those artificial and quasi-legal or quasi-mathematical conceptions of the rule of right and the fitness of things dating from a period that lacked the historical sense, ignored progress, and thought you could lay down a law valid for all times and countries, or even, as Kant said in an extravagance of Trans-cendentalism, not merely for men but for all rational beings in any possible universe.

It will be admitted that the outcome of the age in which this "realistic" current, with its collective "will to" one thing or the other as the ultimate reason, arrived at its culmination, has not exactly been such as to condemn in advance a reconsideration of the question whether the first business of moral philosophy is not to establish a law eternally valid. I do not wish, however, to put it rhetorically, but scientifically. It seems to me demonstrable that, while the reaction against the most typical statements of the "absolute" ethics of moral law were in a measure justified, the great step taken by ethics in modern times has been to give more abstract clearness to the statement of law as distinguished from end. This transition, as it appears in the same age, so also resembles in character the transition from the "synthetic" geometry of the ancients to the analytical geometry of Descartes. It is not in the least that ancient ethics is like ancient geometry, or that modern abstract ethics is like modern analytical geometry; but there is a resemblance of relations. In both cases a definite step was taken to a higher degree of abstraction.

The true founder of modern abstract ethics did not belong to the line of thinkers classed as "Apriorists," but to the line of the great English Experientialists. His ultimate foundation of ethics was not, indeed, finally adequate. The only way in which it could be made adequate was by principles expressly stated against him in his own time by embittered opponents; but in effect he had framed a new and more abstract conception that could not permanently be lost. It was indeed the very clearness with which he had defined his conception that showed his principles to be insufficient.

Thus Descartes was not wrong when, displeased as he was with Hobbes's criticisms of his metaphysics, he saw in him the promise of a new power in the moral sciences. For the *De Cive* (published in 1642) was in reality the outline of a new demonstrative method in ethics comparable for revolutionary importance to Descartes's *Method* and *Meditations* in metaphysics. As in the case of Descartes, there had been a long preparation in the intermediate period for this sudden apparition of a new way of stating fundamental problems. The preparation for Descartes's primary reference of the problem of knowledge to the consciousness of the thinker, consisted in the precision given by long scholastic manipulation to conceptions arrived at in the last period of ancient thought. The preparation for Hobbes's ethics and politics was the similar scholastic manipulation of the generalised positions underlying the later Roman law as put into form under influences from philosophy. Here also that which had been arrived at as a result, and had in the meantime been forced within an alien framework, was now liberated and became a new beginning with not yet revealed possibilities of future application.

It is remarkable that the titles of the three divisions of the *De Cive*—"Libertas," "Imperium," "Religio"—correspond respectively to the predominant elements in what had been till then the three chief phases in the past historical development of Europe, viz., Greek and Italian city-State; Macedonian and Roman Empire; Christian Theocracy. Probably this was not in Hobbes's mind. The order for him was not an order in time but a rational order. His theoretical scheme was intended as an analysis of the elements in all States; and of course in the history of Europe from classical antiquity onward we do not find any of the elements absent at any stage. Yet there are differences of degree. An ancient city-State undoubtedly included dominion and religion; but to us liberty seems relatively predominant in it as compared with the later political order of antiquity. So, in the next stage, autocracy did not exclude all liberty, and it sought aid in the revival of religion; but the dominion of the monarch as representing the State remains characteristic. Again, under theocracy there were recognised private and municipal liberties, and it could not subsist without empire or monarchy; but what seems to us characteristic is religion newly-organised as a power for systematically controlling human life.

Hobbes's age had been preceded by the break-down of this; and his political interest lay in showing the necessity of "Imperium"—the dominion of the national States of the new Europe, best centralised, he thought, in national monarchies—as the means of control. Primitive liberty is an anarchy that has to be overcome; and religion, as he knew it in his time, seemed to him a principle of strife hostile to civil order. For all that, he finds it possible to found ethics rationally, though not to get it into action, in an assumed state of anarchy. Men are imagined as at first relatively isolated beings, seeking their own good, but under no settled government. This state of "liberty" thus means in practice "war of all against all." Yet there is a natural or moral law discernible by human intelligence, though in the state of war no one can consistently keep it, because no one can have security that it will be observed by others reciprocally. Here, it has not been sufficiently observed,

Hobbes sets himself free at the outset alike from metaphysical and naturalistic fallacy, from political and
theological "heteronomy." His own conception of moral
or natural law is carefully distinguished both from law
in the sense of "uniformity of nature" and from law in
the sense of command by a political superior or a supernatural ruler. Laws of nature in the ethical sense he
defines as "certain conclusions understood by reason, concerning things to be done and left undone[1]." The moral
law is the rule which all ought to have the intention
and to make the effort to observe whenever its observance
becomes possible. It is "natural" not as consisting in
conformity to certain physical (any more than metaphysical) realities, but as ascertainable by the reason
natural to men without other aid. In order that the
moral law may be actually observed, what is necessary
is the security given by a government. This may be
democratic, aristocratic or monarchical. When it is constituted, the duty of obedience to it becomes paramount;
for only in the state of peace as opposed to the state of
war can there be observance of the moral law. Because
the law cannot be observed without it, a dictate of the
law of nature is to seek peace, and, having obtained it,
not to lapse into the state of war. Fundamentally the
law of nature, the observance of which the State now
makes possible, is the law of justice, summed up in such
precepts as, to render to each his own, to keep contracts,
not to do to another what we would not that another
should do to us. Thus we have passed from an unrestricted liberty of all to do anything, which was of

---

[1] *De Cive*, iii. 33: "conclusiones quaedam ratione intellectae, de
agendis et omittendis."

no value to anyone precisely because it was unrestricted, to a dominion of one man or of an assembly (either limited to a class or including the whole people or its representatives), which by the restraint of law makes secure certain "rights" that are the residue of primitive liberty. To "natural religion"—the religion that might have been arrived at by human reason—Hobbes regards the notion of a moral government of the universe as essential: for it, the moral laws become divine commands. Such a natural religion would have offered no difficulty to the civil State, of which it would simply have confirmed the legislation so far as this was in accordance with natural law[1]; but, in dealing with actual religion, he was confronted with the rival claims of every clergy to enforce its own version of the Judaeo-Christian revelation as a power above all States. His method of dealing with these was not directly to propose that the State should refuse to recognise any but natural religion; though he made an approach to this in setting forth a much reduced account of what the revelation might be construed to mean. The position for which with all his strength he contended was that no coercive authority on behalf of any religion, and no power of judging what

[1] I do not think it is possible to know Hobbes's ultimate thought about religion; but I seem to find a reserve in favour of the possible truth of ethical theism.

In the famous definitions of *Leviathan* (Part i, chap. 6) he was of course indulging his humour, deliberately accentuating what gave scandal in his exaltation of the State. "*Feare* of power invisible, feigned by the mind, or imagined from tales publiquely allowed, RELIGION; not allowed, SUPERSTITION."

In *De Cive* (xvi. 1) he is at least not obviously ironical when he describes superstition as having its source in "fear without right reason"; atheism, in "the opinion of reason, without fear."

it meant, should be exercised by any but the civil magis-
trate. Ultimately, for religion as for everything else,
there must be a power in the State with which the final
decision rests, and there can be no separation of powers.
In a commonwealth where a priesthood rules, the
ultimate power rests with it in religion also because it
is in effect itself the civil government, not because it has
any rights as against the State.

Now what interests us at present in Hobbes's ethico-
political system is to know whence came historically its
distinctively ethical element. It has already become
evident that, in spite of his absolutism, he has to derive
it from the state of liberty. Only thus could he make
his morality really autonomous. But, to determine how
autonomous morality had come to be the ideal, we must
review the historical series of political types.

Beginning at the beginning, even those whose political
sympathies are with Hobbes's republican contemporaries
must admit that the city-republics of Greece had some of
the disadvantages of liberty as it exists in the state of
nature, before there are laws. Relatively to modern
governments, their governments were weak, and inade-
quate to preserve order. They were torn by factions
compared with which the political parties of modern
times represent very mild differences. Most important of
all, small as they were they could not, even when confronted with an outer world of much greater magnitude
and of inferior civilisation, arrive at any permanent
agreement to avoid war among themselves. Through
Macedon and afterwards through Rome (which under its
aristocratic Republic had coordinated Italy) government
became stronger and civil security increased if liberty

in its good as well as in its bad sense decayed. The
common rule of many cities and provinces, under Rome
as under Macedon, was found in the long run impracticable
except by a peculiar combination of "Imperium" and
"Religio." The new imperial monarchs, beginning with
Alexander, revived from the dead or dying religions of
Babylon and Egypt the idea of the king as divine in-
carnation[1]. When a new revealed religion arose, and the
system of the Roman Empire passed into a theocracy,
the king or emperor ruled, no longer indeed as a "god
manifest," but as the vicegerent of the supreme God.
And, when the Empire, under barbarian impact, broke
into fragments, the separated theocratic power (as Hobbes
himself noted) seemed to hold dominion as the ghost of
the no longer existent unity. It would thus be obvious,
and not long since it would have been fashionable to say,
See how beneficent and how indispensable are force and
illusion! Yet it would not have been the deepest truth.
Whatever the world owes to these powers, it does not
owe to them the essential thing in ethics.

Of this, though of course nothing exactly like his
"state of nature" ever existed, the historic origin was
not unlike that which was postulated by Hobbes. In the
ancient cities there was, as everywhere among men, the
pursuit of ends, which for simplicity may be considered,
as Hobbes considered it, egoistic. This was regulated by
customary laws (νόμοι), about the origin of which it
must be left to anthropologists to form conjectures.

[1] See, for a history of the process in the case of the Macedonian
monarchies, *Greek Imperialism* (1913), by Professor W. Scott Ferguson.
I cannot, however, follow the writer in admitting an important influence
from Aristotle in Alexander's assumption of divinity.

Whatever this may have been, they could not retain their sanctity in a world where there was constant comparison with different customary laws and constant discussion among ingenious minds occupied with moral and political questions. Meanwhile, the philosophers thought out moral systems in relation to their conceptions of the true good of man; but evidently these could not dominate whole communities. Thus we are confronted with the phenomena of dissolution usually ascribed to decay of belief. But, while customary law and ethics had been breaking down and the philosophic schools had only been able to construct systems for a few to live by, the result of the existence of free States with their deliberative assemblies and their law courts, in which also the method was debate, had been the evolution of another kind of law whereby the inevitable conflicts of interest among individuals pursuing their own good were adjusted according to norms that all could recognise as applicable. This process, begun in Greece, was more systematically carried forward by the Roman jurists. As historians allow, its basis was essentially laid under the Roman Republic. Under the monarchy, the original impulse having been given before, development could go on by deductive logic and consultation of precedents. Thus, when free political life had ceased, the autocrat became the organ of the moral law implicit in the legal codes. That this was the real value of the monarchy was pointed out by later philosophers, who regarded it as in this respect replacing the want of sufficient virtue in the multitude. As has been already suggested, this view is quite in accordance with the essential thought of Hobbes; though it would not have suited his polemical purpose to put it exactly in that way. For Hobbes, conceiving the moral law as a system of rules capable of being worked out, though not applied, by rational men even in a state of anarchy, never anywhere treats either government or religion as the creator of morality. In his view, one who observes the law only because of punishments or rewards, whether natural or supernatural, is not truly moral.

Doubtless in this historical development the conception of justice had become in a manner externalised. When, in the statement of the moral law, the command of a sovereign, human or divine, was placed at the summit, and "sanctions" were brought constantly into view as the means of enforcing it in the absence of inward disposition; when, moreover, freedom of discussion was limited to deductions from what was given; it is evident that we can no longer expect such impressive appeals to eternal right as we find in the Attic drama. Yet the real spring of the development was in the self-evidence of this inward law beyond sanctions; and Hobbes, in spite of his paradoxes in laying down the duty of unqualified obedience to the sovereign, has as clear a view of it essentially as any one. Nowhere did he make this clearer than when he expressly put another selected formula by the side of a formula authorised by religion. It may seem, he says, at first sight difficult to know whether any proposed action is or is not in accordance with the laws of nature, these having been deduced by an artificial process from their tendency to our conservation. There is, however, an easy rule. Let any one, when in doubt whether that which he is about to do to another is in accordance with natural law or not, conceive himself in that other's place.

"Atque haec regula non modo facilis, sed etiam dudum celebrata his verbis est, *quod tibi fieri non vis, alteri ne feceris*[1]." Here he deliberately chooses the negative form of the law of reciprocity (found for example in Isocrates): "Do not to another what you would not that another should do to you." The positive form given in the Gospel (Matt. vii. 12), he remarks[2], is "almost in the same words" (totidem pene verbis); thus dissociating the precept of natural justice from any intrinsic dependence on a divine command. The rule that we are to keep our contracts is similarly made prior to the pact or covenant into which the chosen people of God was said to enter. The promise in Deuteronomy[3] made by the people to observe the law of Moses is treated as a particular case of a contract, the meaning and obligations of which are to be determined by an application of the general principles of natural justice. The law, to love your neighbour as yourself, that is, as Hobbes interprets it, to recognise his equal right, to imagine yourself in his place when you are free from passion, existed even before Moses: "for it is the natural law, having its beginning with the rational nature itself[4]."

Thus Hobbes's conception of morality, as Croom

[1] *De Cive*, iii. 26.
[2] *Ibid.*, iv. 23.
[3] Hobbes anticipated the whole course of Biblical criticism from Spinoza onward to the most recent schools in declaring Deuteronomy the earliest book of the Law (*De Cive*, xvi. 12).
[4] *De Cive*, xvii. 8.   Cf. xvii. 13, where the distinction is still more expressly drawn between the teaching of justice and observation of the natural laws "ut theoremata per rationem naturalem; deducendo jus et leges naturales a principiis contractibusque humanis" and "ut leges per auctoritatem divinam, ostendendo talem esse voluntatem Dei."

Robertson has said[1], does not exclude "anything that
the consciousness of mankind recognises as duty or
virtue in the individual." Altruism as a spring of
obedience to the moral law is on occasion recognised[2].
"Right reason," on which his contemporary opponents
took their stand, is constantly declared to be existent
prior to positive law. Although the supreme power,
once constituted, is absolute, and no right of rebellion
can be recognised in subjects, yet it is the duty of those
who hold the supreme power to obey right reason[3]. The
ethical laws of nature are immutable and eternal[4]. Even
between States they remain valid as "divine law," though
they cannot be enforced[5]. How then was it that his
system became for a time so discredited morally?

The causes were not entirely inherent in the real
character of the system. Unfairness and prejudice were
not absent even in an opponent of high philosophic power

[1] *Hobbes*, p. 143.

[2] *De Cive*, xviii. 3: "qui amant proximum, non possunt non velle
obedire legi morali, quae consistit, ut supra capite tertio ostensum
est, in *superbiae, ingratitudinis, contumeliae, inhumanitatis, inclementiae,
injuriae* similiumque offensarum prohibitione, quibus proximi laeduntur."

[3] *Ibid.*, xiii. 2: "*officii* tamen eorum est rectae rationi, quae lex est
naturalis moralis et divina, quantum possunt in omnibus obedire."

[4] *Ibid.*, iii. 29: "Leges naturae *immutabiles* et *aeternae* sunt: quod
vetant, nunquam licitum esse potest: quod jubent, nunquam illici-
tum."

[5] *Ibid.*, xiv. 5: "*Humana lex* omnis civilis est. Nam extra civi-
tates status hominum hostilis est; in quo, quia alter alteri non sub-
jicitur, leges praeter dictamina rationis naturalis, quae lex divina est,
nullae sunt." Hobbes's exclusion of the thought of an international
law is thus less absolute than Spinoza's (see *Tractatus Politicus*, iii.
13, 14). Spinoza, on the other hand, in incorporating the general
positions of Hobbes, makes clear, as Hobbes did not, the limits beyond
which a tyrannic power will find itself unable to enforce civil obedience
within the State.

like Cudworth. Yet it remains true that Hobbes could not ultimately justify his own conception of virtue and duty in their inwardness by the reasons he gives. Justice, in his view, is most certainly not merely prudence; yet, if it could be explained wholly on his principles as the means adapted to the end he assigns, that is what it would be reduced to. It is of course quite true that the enforcement of certain rules of justice by the State is the means to "peace and defence," and that it is on the whole to the interest of every individual that the State should be strong enough to enforce them. Thus Hobbes, by assuming a primeval conflict of egoistic interests, and by supposing men rational enough to seek a way of adjusting the perpetual strife that would otherwise go on, can furnish a ground for the construction of a commonwealth and its laws. If, however, we put the case as it concerns the individual, and ask why any person should observe the rule when he can clearly see that in the particular case it is not to his interest and can be evaded with impunity, what is the answer simply from the point of view of the only ultimate end theoretically admitted, viz., egoistic interest? A later way of meeting the objection on Hobbes's experientialist principles was by means of a modified psychology, in which more account is taken than by Hobbes of the altruistic elements in human nature as a normal, and not merely exceptional and incalculable, spring of action. But suppose these to exist in fact, in what consists even then the strict obligation to observe the moral law? Hobbes and his contemporaries, being in general "intellectualists," would have at once admitted the validity of Kant's argument against founding ethics simply on benevolence; that no

one can be obliged to feel in a certain way. In fact
Hobbes had put this in his own manner: the moral
obligation is to an action, or, from the internal and more
properly ethical point of view, to an intention and effort,
not to a feeling. The question then is, whether a person
has not strictly a right on Hobbes's principles, should he
happen to be in feeling a pure egoist, to ignore the interests
of the commonwealth in every case where they do not
include his own. And we must not of course suppose
a mere blunderer, who is sure to overreach himself, but
a man of insight who sees his way clear to profitable
injustice. It was in considerations of this kind that
Cudworth's attack on Hobbes's moral and political
system was ultimately based. No doubt he had in view
the dramatic representation of this type of thinking
by Plato, and its attempted self-justification by ideas
superficially resembling those of Hobbes. His own aim
was to place the moral law above everything even in
appearance arbitrary. As a Platonising theologian, he
held the intellect to be prior to the will of God. The
moral law is a divine command because it is right; it is
not right because commanded. Similarly political command is in the second place in relation to the law of
justice as intellectually discerned. Now although this,
if we look closely, is in effect conceded by Hobbes, his
system certainly gave a different impression. It seemed
as if justice in his view was finally identical with the will
of the State, and even as if the State could make a
doctrine true or false, in the only meaning those words
can practically bear, at its arbitrary will. Some of this
was deliberate paradox to strike the public mind; and
undoubtedly it had that effect. On one side it was

regarded with real or assumed horror; and on the other side a kind of "immoralism," having for its watchword "power," like that with which we have become recently familiar, took pleasure in calling itself "Hobbism." Thus historically the reaction of Cudworth and the Cambridge Platonists was justified, and we have to inquire more exactly what it meant and how far it succeeded or failed.

Essentially it meant that the moral law, conceived as a law of justice, is ultimately *a priori*. This could be argued without great difficulty from the concessions of Hobbes, who indeed anticipated the title of Cudworth's *Treatise concerning Eternal and Immutable Morality* in what he says himself of the moral law; which is for him also, as we have seen, an immutable and eternal law of right reason. It was only necessary to show that the experiential ground is insufficient. Now the sufficiency of Hobbes's proof *a posteriori*, apart from external criticism, is quite invalidated by incidental remarks of his own; such as, that animals "non distinguunt injuriam a damno[1]," and that men are so difficult to govern precisely because they do make this distinction. For it necessarily follows that the distinction is not a consequence of the command of a political superior. If then, in spite of the fact that all education in the principles of social justice is and must be an affair of authorised tradition, the idea of injustice as distinguished from loss or damage can nevertheless be turned against the State itself, how, it may be asked, can this idea be other than *a priori*? For it is quite inexplicable as a mere subjective fancy of particular minds. The notion of having suffered in-justice in a particular case may, it is true, be a mere

[1] *De Cive*, v. 5.

fancy; but there remains irremovable the constant
possibility of appeal to this generalised idea under which
alone the particular case becomes arguable. Morality,
then, is ultimately irreducible to a balance of gain and
loss. Underivable, as we saw, from direct egoistic calculation, it is also underivable mediately from political
command.

In the polemic of the Cambridge Platonists, however,
the purely ethical criticism of Hobbes's foundation of
morals was never quite disentangled from the metaphysical criticism of his mechanical or "corporealist"
system of speculative doctrine. With Cudworth's successor Samuel Clarke, the same attachment of the moral
law to the idea of theoretical truth remained. Both
alike were unable to escape, as Hobbes had already
escaped, from the "metaphysical fallacy." Hobbes regarded his "civil philosophy" as capable of standing on
its basis in the doctrine of human nature, without reference to the mechanical philosophy which formed the first
part of the complete system he had planned and partly
worked out. They, on the contrary, thought that, to
provide a basis for their ethics, they must first overthrow
materialism and establish a spiritualist metaphysic on
principles of pure reason. Hence Cudworth, in particular, spent most of his force on preliminaries. Not
only must materialism in all its phases be refuted so
far as it claimed to give an account of the whole; but at
the same time the "true intellectual system of the
universe" must incorporate what was sound in the
physical doctrine of ancient and modern atomists. On
another side there was rising a new Protagorean sub-
jectivism, denying all knowledge as distinguished from

opinion. This too must be refuted, as Plato had set himself to refute Protagoras. The general result was, not indeed a mere waste of power, for Cudworth's work had effect, but certainly an expenditure of thought and learning that on the whole seemed to miss the mark through over-elaborateness. Though he was undoubtedly driving at the thought of an "autonomous ethics," he did not succeed in getting it adequately formulated. It was with him an original thought, stimulated by opposition to Hobbes and going beyond what had been expressed by his Neo-Platonic masters; but, while the moral law was by him set definitely against self-interest or arbitrary will, he had not arrived at a clear understanding that it was independent of intellectual truth about being. On the metaphysical side he was more definitely than in ethics a disciple rather than a discoverer; so that it was left to Berkeley to find a more modern way against the "corporealists." In ethics, his direction was followed in England only by thinkers of the second order. The next effective step towards founding the type of doctrine to which he had aspired was not taken before Kant.

During the eighteenth century, new development was given, in the systems called utilitarian, to the doctrine that makes ends supreme. Partly in subordination and partly in opposition to this general doctrine, various investigations were carried forward in the psychology of ethics, as distinguished from ethics proper. Usually with Hobbes in view as an opponent, the disinterested and benevolent as contrasted with the selfish elements in human nature were brought out. Theories of "moral sense," "conscience," "sympathy," were set against the doctrines that tended to make moral conduct an affair of calculation. So in later times we have had theories of "intuition," ascribing merit to an action according to the psychological rank of the motive from which it proceeds. All these doctrines have their value and interest, for all start from the description of something that exists in human nature, however they may explain it; but none could seriously compete with Utilitarianism in the claim to furnish a standard. All the principles, including conscience, the most impressive, have the fault that they are "subjective" in the sense of varying from individual to individual. No doubt we ought to obey conscience; but how are we to form our conscience? Of the origin of conscience, theories are endless.

> Love is too young to know what conscience is;
> Yet who knows not conscience is born of love?

That is one theory, and it may be regarded as the zenith; but actual consciences are very varied, and no doubt it would be true to say that some have their spring in fear. Conscience therefore, like the other principles referred to, belongs to "anthropology" in Kant's sense. He was not without interest in this; and he did not at all deny the merits of the psychological moralists of his century; but he could find in them no solution of his own problem, which he had clearly conceived as that of finding a rational *a priori* law. Of the major systems that had preceded his own, that of Hume is of course in principle entirely governed by the idea of end. It was by his criticism of metaphysics and theology, not by his ethics of "benevolent utilitarianism," that Hume influenced Kant. This type of doctrine Kant had constantly in view, but simply as a type, not in its subtleties. To him it was the great opposing doctrine, which it was his aim to supersede.

To understand the essential principles of Kant's ethics, the best book to read is the *Grundlegung zur Metaphysik der Sitten* (1785), which he wrote before the *Kritik der praktischen Vernunft* (1788) in order to dispose in advance of certain strictly scientific questions. The *Practical Reason* is properly an episodic treatise on metaphysics in so far as determined by ethics. The later *Metaphysik der Sitten* (1797)[1] is a return to the details of ethics in greater complexity, and in effect set free from all attachment to any speculative position.

For the title *Metaphysic of Morals* must not mislead us. Kant was as free from the "metaphysical" as from the "naturalistic" fallacy. And he was free consciously. By "metaphysic of ethics" he did not mean a speculative doctrine about reality, on which the theory of practice was to be founded, but a "first philosophy" of ethics itself, bringing out the principles essential to the constitution of any rational system of morals. Thus he made a genuinely new departure; for, while some others had been free from the actual fallacies, no one before had set himself to realise, in deliberate contrast to everything else, the idea of what ought to be, independently alike of the physical sciences, of anthropology and of theology.

Kant holds his ethical doctrine to be true on any supposition whatever as to the constitution of the universe. It is as true on the hypothesis of atheism as of theism; though in the *Critique of Practical Reason* it is made the ground for postulating theism. It is as true for

---

[1] Comprising the *Metaphysische Anfangsgründe der Rechtslehre* and the *Metaphysische Anfangsgründe der Tugendlehre*.

all other rational beings, if any exist, as for men. If we start from the matter of the will, the *end*, and not from its form, the *law*, then there are no metaphysical principles of ethics; but the theory of virtue is then corrupted at its source[1]. The true basis of ethics is thought, not feeling. What we have to aim at is the statement of certain universal maxims for the conduct of all rational beings. The supreme maxim cannot be merely hypothetical: Act in such and such a way if you desire a certain end (say, the happiness of mankind). It must be categorical. The first form in which Kant states it is the famous "categorical imperative": Act according to the maxim that can at the same time be made universal law.

After more than a century of discussion, the verdict of criticism seems to be that this is too purely formal to enable us to proceed to any propositions whatever relating to ends. Yet Kant's system, in his own view, stands or falls according as this passage is or is not practicable. From the form of the moral law, we must be able to arrive at propositions that can positively determine actual conduct in its ends. If this were true without qualification, I think we should have to conclude that Kant's ethical doctrine has failed, for no ends are deducible from mere formal law. I have indicated, however, in what manner his position seems to me to remain valid. We must recognise that the moral law could not exist at all except for beings pursuing ends, and that these ends can be determined only by experience. The moral law therefore implies them, and does not assign them. But, if the ends cannot be deduced from the law,

[1] *Metaphysische Anfangsgründe der Tugendlehre*, Vorrede.

neither can the law, in all its stringency, be deduced from the ends. This stringency is finally inexplicable from pure experience.

On the other hand, Kant's "pure will" or "good will," considered formally as the mere will to obey the moral law, can by itself determine no action whatever. Utilitarianism, in the generalised sense that some good is the end, is the necessary method for determining actual conduct. We must recognise this openly, not bring in utilitarian considerations surreptitiously, as Kant does in trying to construct a working system for the life of man out of pure forms.

Even as a formal principle, Kant's categorical imperative seems to me to retain little value. Professor Juvalta (whose criticism will be found set forth in more detail in the next chapter) makes the observation, which is exactly to the point, that it fails to exclude some modes of life generally regarded as immoral, and would exclude some that are admitted to be moral, whatever other objection might be taken to them. For the ruthless pursuit of power is quite compatible with the maxim, provided you do not complain when beaten, while the mode of life of St Francis of Assisi is not. One of the Kantian maxims, however, he allows, does go beyond a mere empty formalism. Now this, while itself formal, complies with the condition stated above. Making no end part of the maxim, it yet recognises that man as the subject of the moral law is a being pursuing ends. So act (the maxim runs) as to treat humanity, in thy own person as well as in the person of every other, always at the same time as an end, never as a mere means.

This formula, Kant himself insists, is much more than

"the trivial, *quod tibi non vis fieri*, etc."; for under it
positive duties can be brought, as they cannot be brought
under a merely negative formula[1]. This might lead to
a good deal of dialectic. First it could be remarked
that the law of contradiction also is negative and may be
called trivial; but that no one save a philosopher ever
seriously tries to carry it through the various portions
of his thinking in their mutual relations; and that no
system of philosophy that exists has been able to bear
its thoroughgoing application. Still, it could be said in
reply that the law of contradiction, though necessary, is
not sufficient to constitute even a system of logic, let
alone a system of philosophy; and that similarly, the
negative form of the law of reciprocity, though necessary,
is not sufficient even to make action formally right.
Without further discussion I am myself ready to admit
that Kant's maxim regarding the mutual respect of
persons for one another as ends and not mere means is
well entitled to a place of its own as a classical expression
of the idea of justice for a society in which freedom is
explicitly recognised. The negative formula selected by
Hobbes, applying to societies of all types, has less content.
The corresponding positive formula, Do to others as you
would that others should do to you, is of course logically
no more than equivalent to the negative formula. I
think it has been said with truth that whenever it appears
to mean more it is wrong. Gibbon found the negative
maxim (from Isocrates) the most apt to quote against
religious persecution. Certainly it would be more difficult
to reconcile in appearance with the negative than with the

[1] *Grundlegung zur Metaphysik der Sitten* (*Werke*, Berlin, G. Reimer, Bd. iv. 1903, p. 430 note).

positive formula that which has been called "persecution from love[1]."

If Kant himself prefers the apparently most universalised maxim, called distinctively the categorical imperative, to a maxim that recognises explicitly the existence of ends, this, I think, characterises the attempt to do more with pure form than will ever be possible. The merit of the second maxim is that, while it still has the formal character of *a priori* law, it points to the kind of matter (that is, the ends of persons), though not to any particular matter, to which it is applicable. A third formulation, in which it is laid down that moral legislation must be imposed by the will on itself (autonomy as against heteronomy) serves to bring out still more clearly the conditions of a moral personality. The instability of Kant's own position in so far as it claims to be pure rationalism is revealed when he says: How pure reason can be for itself practical, that is, how the mere principle of the universal validity of all its maxims as laws, without any materially interesting object of the will, can itself bring into operation a purely moral interest, no human reason can explain[2]. The solution, I have already suggested, is that there is nothing precisely of this kind for it to explain. All rational action is and must be with a view to ends thought as goods. The abstract moral law, which is the law of justice, is a limiting condition in the pursuit of ends. That is how the recognition of it modifies action; not by the determination of a special class of positive actions that may be called moral in distinction

---

[1] Whether this aberration of benevolence ever existed I express no opinion. A magnificent representation of it is to be found in Victor Hugo's *Torquemada*.   [2] *Loc. cit.* p. 461.

from others. Even the special aim of promoting public
justice—the aim of the kings and rulers beatified in
Dante's Heaven of Jupiter—is simply a mode of the
fulfilment of duty in a given position: it is not more
moral in itself, though it may be nobler or more meritorious, than any other fulfilment. What always determines a rational action is the notion of a good for oneself
or others. The enforcement of justice, for example,
may be regarded as a good for the commonwealth, and
to promote it as a form of altruism. Any action, whether
altruistic or egoistic, and whether positively meritorious
or not, may be called moral when it does not infringe the
laws of justice, conceived of course in the ethical and not
merely in the legal sense. This last condition is included
in the condition formulated by Kant as the autonomy in
distinction from the heteronomy of the will. Materially
a merely legal and a moral action may be the same; but
an action performed because of external compulsion has
not the character of a moral action properly so-called.
Here, at least, all moralists are in agreement.

What remains of Kant's *a priori* method is the recognition that the supreme ethical maxims, though by themselves insufficient to determine a positive code of conduct,
have a validity that no deduction from ends could confer
on them. The law of justice is not a mere means to any
good whatever; though action in accordance with it is
undoubtedly a means to the greatest goods. Hence the
utilitarian arguments for the observance of justice have
always been felt, even by those who could think of nothing
better, to be an imperfect reply to objections put in the
mouths of imaginary sophistical casuists. They seemed
too much like the maintenance of a mere general rule,

once fixed by prescription, against the insight of science or direct intuition. And it is not only egoism, but frequently altruism, that rises up against the rules of justice. I need only mention benevolent schemes founded on biology that involve treating the human race as a herd. Yet, as I have admitted, on no theory are all cases perfectly simple. How the rules of justice affect actual conduct will be considered when we come to discuss further the relation of abstract to concrete ethics. Meanwhile, a few words must be said on the formalism of Kant in relation to developments since his time.

Whether for disciples or opponents, this has been the most impressive thing in Kant's ethics. The whole complex system no one has ever accepted in its entirety; and, avowedly or not, the preliminary alike to following and to criticising has always been artificial simplification. This was the method of Hegel; who, in putting forth all his power to show the want of content in Kant's formalism, dealt with it as the most thoroughgoing utilitarian might have done. Thus Hegel may be taken as typical of Kant's critics.

His own doctrine, at the summit, is a doctrine of the end or highest good, not of *a priori* law. The Hegelian formula, "self-realisation," undoubtedly includes a regard for personality absent from what is thought to be typical utilitarianism, with its "hedonical calculus"; but, after all, self-realisation is a formula of the Art of Life, not of Abstract Ethics. In my view, it is a very good formula in its own sphere; but it does not solve, but evades, the real question raised by Kant. Of course it is not necessarily an egoistic formula, and is not in the least

incompatible with Comte's precept, "Live for others[1]."
The individual, for Hegel as for Comte, is in his very
nature social; a temporary embodiment of history, an
"abstraction" from the real being which is Humanity.
Self-realisation is realisation of the individual as at the
same time an organ of society. But, if we were to deal with
Hegel on the method of simplification applied to Kant,
we should have to say that justice is not a valid concept
in his system at all. The ultimate test of right is Fact.
Creon is as much, and as little, justified as Antigone.
The right of both is at once affirmed and cancelled in
the process that brings into collision the two elements in
human life summed up as the Family and the State.
Here the only reply is that, whatever this fancy may be
worth, it leaves the problem of justice unsolved; and
that we have the poet on our side. Sophocles leaves us
in no doubt that he regards the right as with Antigone,
and he suggests no solution such as Hegel's[2]. The problem,
how far justice is also fact, remains a problem. To an
Athenian audience, as to us, right was clearer than
ultimate fact. And certainly the Fact that is identical
with appearance was not the moral judge.

But, as Kant was not in reality a pure formalist, but
has much to say that takes full account of fact in concrete
cases, so Hegel was not in reality the mere worshipper of

[1] Kant himself had generalised the ends in the rival systems of ethics
before him in the two formulae: "one's own perfection" and "others'
happiness." Both of these he claimed to deduce as elements in his own
doctrine.

[2] An effect of Hegel's criticism has been that for English classical
scholarship Creon has become an embodiment of the Prussian State.
To an Athenian contemporary of Sophocles, this of course would have
meant not an embodiment of one relative right against another, but of
arbitrary despotism against the autonomy of the "good will."

present fact that he seemed in his conservative moods to his revolutionary contemporaries. Fact is ultimately Thought; and Thought, evolving in history and its highest products, which include systems of morality, is only through a process not yet completed the judge of all things. The final judgment has not been passed till the highest expressions of the process have appeared. This at any rate seems to me a fair interpretation; but I confess that I am criticising systems of which I am not singular in finding the external form repellent. Even Kant's system, it will scarcely be denied by his most devoted disciples, is an ultra-Gothic edifice; though Kant belongs to the small number of thinkers of whom it can be said that in sheer power they have no superior. But philosophy, in spite of a common prejudice; is a progressive thing. And no degree of difficulty in really profound thought has ever prevented its complete assimilation by the European intellect. Of this the historical destiny of Aristotle's *Metaphysics* is a sufficient proof. Thus it was to be expected that the insight in Kant's Ethics would sooner or later pass on, not without progress, into a construction in some simpler style of architecture. This expectation has been realised by the publication of Professor Juvalta's book, which I now proceed to expound.

CHAPTER V

THE SOLUTION OF JUVALTA[1]

Professor Juvalta expressly distinguishes the old and the new problem of morality as the problem of modern ethics before and after Kant. The old problem was to find the foundation of a morality about the content of which there was agreement. The new problem is to determine whether there are "values" specifically moral. It is not new in the rigorous sense, for it was also the problem of pre-Christian ethics; but it differs by discarding the ancient presupposition that the moral good must necessarily be a form of happiness.

To anticipate: it seeks the law instead of the end, but requires that it should be intrinsic, an expression of autonomy, not imposed by external authority.

For expounding Professor Juvalta's work, the simplest way has seemed to me to be the most straightforward. I shall follow his chapters and headings, and shall almost limit myself to exposition without comment[2].

[1] *Il Vecchio e il Nuovo Problema della Morale.* By E. Juvalta. Bologna: N. Zanichelli, 1914.

[2] One remark must be made on the translation of the word "coscienza." I have rendered it by "conscience" or "consciousness" as seemed convenient. It has no special significance for Juvalta's doctrine, which is not a form of what used to be called Intuitionism, but of Rationalism modified by contact with empirical theories of ethics.

I.

THE FOUNDATION OF MORALITY.

1. *The Character of the Problem and its Forms.* The problem is fictitious, for there is no foundation outside morality itself. Precisely for this reason, the dictates of the moral conscience have not been accepted or rejected according as they agreed or did not agree with ethical systems, but, on the contrary, these have been accepted or rejected according as they seemed adapted or unadapted to furnish the ground for moral convictions.

In fact, four types of solution have been put forward. I. To consider moral principles as "truths," of which the foundation is sought in a reality objectively given to consciousness.   II. To demonstrate the goodness of that which morality prescribes, that is, to derive its norms from an end or from a good or order of goods.   III. To prove its authority, founded either (A) in History, or (B) in a Will distinct from the personal will and imposing itself on this.

2. *The Foundation sought in the Reality.* The theoretical foundation is equally illusory whether it is sought in "science" or in "metaphysics."   For clearly, since thinkers of equal good faith, and whose logical competence can only be denied by a *petitio principii*, connect the same moral criterion with different and opposed theoretical principles, the proof fails that it is necessarily connected with either to the exclusion of the other.   But whence springs the illusion?

On the side of science, it springs from the fallacy of

seeking the way to certain results while leaving unproved the implication that those results are desirable. By no knowledge of the laws of society can the sociologist prove that civilisation is preferable to barbarism. By no knowledge of the laws of life can the biologist prove that life is worth living. Given a certain instinct or will to live, reasons can be assigned for preferring a certain course of conduct; but without that instinct or will no scientific knowledge avails to determine any action whatever.

What has been said of science applies also to metaphysics, so long as we mean by metaphysics knowledge of an "intelligible" reality in so far as intelligible and not as having value. Thus, to establish orders of being or "degrees of reality" avails nothing unless the conception of being includes that of good. Reality simply as existence has no degrees. The apparent ethical bearing of Platonism and related metaphysical doctrines comes from a synthesis of "reality" and "perfection," of existence and value. But the latter is not given in any metaphysical concept; it is carried over from a practical interest, conscious or not.

When a metaphysical doctrine is commended because adapted to furnish the foundation of "true morality," does not this imply that we already know what true morality is, apart from metaphysics?

3. *The Foundation sought in a Justification from Ends.* The fallacy in the attempts made to translate into a rigorous doctrine the derivation of moral values from some incontestable "highest good" arises from this: that while the essence of a moral value consists in its pre-eminence over other values, it is treated as if it were identical with or definable in terms of one of these other values.

The types may be classed under the heads of Utilitarianism and mystical Religiosity; the ends being respectively Happiness and Holiness.

Let us set aside the familiar criticisms on Utilitarianism, and concede that happiness has a determinate content and is a harmony of assignable goods, including satisfaction of one's own conscience, and that it can be demonstrated that constant observance of moral norms is the sure and indispensable way to obtain it. It would thus have been proved only that the moral values are *also* eudaemonological values, not at all that the moral value of an action consists in its being a means to happiness. The question is not about the practical efficacy of arguments for following the rules of morality, but about their theoretical conclusiveness. "Honesty is the best policy" is not a moral reason for being honest. To admit, with Mill, differences of "quality" in the constituents of happiness, amounts in the end simply to approving or disapproving, in the name of happiness, of that which the moral conscience approves or disapproves[1].

On the second type, the remark is to be made that the consciousness of the religious mystic, though in the form of a confused and not clear perception, contains moral values that could not be drawn from the other elements of the perception if they were not already there. Moreover, they are incorporated as something that could subsist apart, and incorporated for that reason. The mystic conceives as morally perfect the Being he adores;

---

[1] Satisfaction of conscience, it is noted, though a good, is not the end of moral conduct; the end is the realising of that value which the conscience recognises as moral.

but no consciousness could find moral values in God if it did not know them already as values and distinguish them as moral from values of other kinds.

This conclusion is unaffected by doubt raised whether the support of religion is not practically necessary for maintaining a stable morality. The case is analogous to that of Utilitarianism. As there, so here, the executive point of view is extraneous to the properly moral question.

The same general argument applies to mixed systems, such as Theological Utilitarianism (hedonistic interpretation of the religious standard) and the Humanitarian Mysticism of Comte (religious interpretation of the utilitarian standard)[1].

However plausible from the present considerations, it would nevertheless be precipitate to conclude that none of these systems have properly ethical as distinguished from hortatory or pedagogic importance. They do indeed all fail in so far as they look for the reason of the supremacy of moral values in something outside the values themselves; but, as a matter of fact, the different kinds of values, moral and other, are connected in all sorts of ways. For example, that which is the object of a moral valuation, say, sincerity, can be estimated from the point of view of an intellectual or artistic or economic interest. Conversely, that which is the object of a hedonistic or aesthetic or any other valuation, say, riches, art, learning, can be estimated also as a good of moral order. Hence arise complex problems of conciliation, among which perhaps the reconciliation of virtue and happiness is not the most important.

---

[1] It is expressly observed that the Utilitarianism of the latter is altruistic; the egoism of the former is understood.

4. *The Foundation sought in Authority.* The authoritative character of the moral judgment and the imperative form it takes, suggest its derivation from something that transcends consciousness while revealing itself in it. Accordingly, the foundation has been placed in historical titles of nobility or in the will of a sovereign power.

A. *The Historical Foundation.* One form taken by the appeal to history is that of "evolutionary ethics." But in fact we judge of the evolution or selection of ideas and feelings by a criterion independent of the process. That which by the hypothesis is its product decides whether the evolution is morally progressive, regressive or indifferent. It is not because juridical "progress" has abolished torture that we condemn torture; it is because we condemn torture that we recognise in its abolition progress in the development of law. Apart from some criterion of valuation, whatever it may be, there are no "superior" or "inferior" forms of life. In evolutionary ethics such a valuation is necessarily assumed, not educed from the order of evolution itself; as was seen when Spencer brought in the hedonistic criterion of a pure pleasure corresponding to complete adaptation to the environment.

This is no less seen when the evolution is internal and psychical than when it is external and mechanical. Substitute a different scale of values, as Nietzsche did, and what was called by the democrat and the humanitarian moral progress becomes a wretched degeneration. And, when conscience, with its criterion of value, opposes itself to that which at the moment has or seems to have the support of history, it has just as good a case as the actual fact, even from the historical point of view; for history, which withdraws its support to-day, may give it to-morrow. History is conservation and development, but also innovation and opposition: in Hegelian terms, it is one thing only because it is at the same time the other.

Even the history of reflective thought on the ethical problem itself cannot furnish a solution, important as it is for attaining clearness to our own minds. The effort after ethical unification in view of the systems revolves around a content furnished by immediate moral experience, and assumes the validity of certain moral judgments. Moreover, new moral intuitions make their appearance from time to time, not only in the systems elaborated by reflective thinkers but also outside all systematic construction. Such affirmation of new values is not the conclusion of a scientific or philosophical investigation, but a penetration or breaking of the moral consciousness into the current of reflective thought, which does not give them but receives them, illuminates but does not create them.

B. *The Foundation sought in a Will.* In examining the imperative character of moral precepts, a distinction is necessary. To speak of the "ought" or of "duty" as characteristic of the moral valuation is equivocal. The duty is not a duty of estimating, but of conforming the action to the estimation. The moral valuation precedes and justifies the obligation, not *vice versa.*

The peculiarity of the moral valuation is that it implies taking sides against any valuation that opposes it. Hence its recognition exacts a constant attitude of the will. Duty, in so far as it is characteristic of morality, that is, in so far as it is internal and not reducible to the feeling of an external compulsion, is the consciousness of what is demanded by the moral value; it manifests itself in its clearest form when it is in conflict with motives of another nature. Thus moral duty presupposes the moral valuation. There would be no sense in speaking of a duty of recognising moral values to a conscience closed to every ethical valuation; for this would amount to the duty of feeling in a certain manner.

Shall we say then that if there are people "morally deaf" they have no duties? In the ethical, or internal, sense they have none; but they may be under the obligation of acting *as if* they recognised at least those grosser moral values that are susceptible of being presented by external coercion as motives appreciable even by a consciousness non-moral. Now this obligation necessarily implies the reference to a superior power distinct from the individual will. As this power imposes itself in view of an end and in agreement with certain norms, it is conceived as the power of a Will [of the State or of the Deity] that commands the observance of those norms. Evidently, however, this would not suffice to give a reason for duty as internal obligation, even if, by tracing it to its origin, it explained the formation of the sense of duty.

Yet, since the moral will manifests itself as the requirement of the constant subordination of motives antagonistic to morality, it reacts in the form of approval of the external coercive power which by its "sanctions" represses those motives. Thus the power that deserves respect is distinguished from the constringent force that merely has to be submitted to. The command may be limited to a certain sphere of moral values [command of the State], or it may coincide with the moral value itself

[command of the Deity].   In either case, the difference
remains between the attitude of the moral and the non-
moral consciousness.   For the first, it is the moral valuation that causes the obligation to be recognised and
respected.   For the second, it is the obligation that
causes moral values to be recognised: the observance of
the obligation is not internal morality, but external
conformity to certain commands that are worth just as
much as the sanction that accompanies them is worth.

If the distinction between command and valuation
is not overcome even when the two terms are unified in
the conception of an authority at once irresistibly powerful
and indefectibly moral, the more manifestly will it subsist
in all other forms of sanction.   There remain, however,
at least in appearance, two ways of evading the conclusion: either to deny all value to the moral consciousness
as such, and to found every valuation on the power
that posits it at its good pleasure; or to transfer the
criterion of moral valuation from the personal consciousness to some other consciousness, impersonal or collective.

Now the first thesis either fails to answer the question
it purports to answer, since to deny all value to the moral
valuation is not to say whence its authority comes; or
it takes away only in words the distinction, which returns
through every subtlety, between justice and arbitrary
will.   When the Platonic Callicles condemns the laws as
an imposition by the foolish and weak many on the clever
and strong few, his blame implies a moral criterion
superior to force; for he thinks it unjust that the actually
predominant force should overrule the force that *ought to*
prevail.   And in the absolutism of Hobbes, the unlimited
power of the sovereign excludes the moral valuation only

in appearance; the reason for submission to its arbitrary will being that a bad law is better than no law and a tyrannical government than no government.

Of the second thesis, all the forms fail to give anything different from the personal consciousness, to which the authority of the collective consciousness is always reducible. For this has no expression except in the person as an individual manifestation of the social consciousness; which indeed only exists in the individual, the ends of society being such only in so far as they are made such by individual persons. Since it is in individual persons that society becomes conscious, moral values are moral only in so far as they are estimated by the personal consciousness. From the ethical point of view, it is not society that gives value to my moral criterion, but my moral criterion that gives value to society. It is to the ethical judgment of the individual that every social reform appeals, including that which calls itself Socialism. The faith which gives itself that name is in fact a moral ideal having for centre the individual. Collective property (whatever might be its actual effects) is aimed at as a necessary condition for rendering effective the liberty of all, for making of each human individual a true human person.

The subtle and complicated doctrine which makes the State the centre of all moral authority has in part been dealt with in the discussion of the doctrines that find the supreme authority in History or in Power. So far as it occupies a distinct place, the decisive point is this: that the ethical value of the State, even if we assume it to be the ideal State, arises from its being the only adequate organ of the universal ethical will that becomes aware of itself as valid in the personal consciousness. Thus in the rational order the knowledge of the value of the State is derivative.

5. *Inversion of the Problems relative to the Foundation of Morality.* Every effort to derive a moral valuation from something of which the moral value is not already recognised is therefore vain or illusory. Either it does not give what is sought, or it presupposes what its claim is to found. Thus the preceding discussions point to an inversion of the problems. The question is no longer to find the reason of moral values in the reality we know, but to discover whether it is possible to affirm a system of realities in correspondence with the order of moral values; not to fix those values by relation to happiness as an end, but to determine whether happiness is ultimately attainable only by morality; not to educe them from history, but to learn whether history can be read as the realisation of a moral process; not to posit them in relation to what a Will imposes, but to ascertain whether the postulate of a Will that imposes them can be theoretically upheld. In any case, the primacy and independence of moral values remains clearly established.

II.

The Plurality of the Moral Criteria.

1. *Kant's Formal Criterion of Valuation.* The independence of moral values and the impossibility of deducing them from any theoretical speculation was recognised and affirmed in the most explicit manner by Kant. To avoid confusion, however, it must be pointed out that

this recognition of the independence of ethics does not necessarily imply acceptance of the principles and methods of Kant's ethical philosophy.

Mere universality of form in ethical legislation can by itself give no content. Reason is only a principle of consistency, theoretical or practical, and yields no direct, as distinguished from derivative, moral values. The "law of the stronger," for example, if taken in a certain sense, is quite reconcilable with Kant's categorical imperative. If indeed I subjugate others to my arbitrary will when I am stronger, and then cry out because I am myself subjugated when I am weaker, I contradict the precept, So to act that I can will that my maxim should at the same time be made law universal; but if force is in truth to me the highest thing, and I do not complain when I am in turn subdued, there is no contradiction of the rule of universality. Kant's more fecund formula, Act so as to treat humanity, whether in thy own person or in that of another, always at the same time as an end and never merely as a means, has this character of fecundity only in so far as it gives a content to the universal; and this content is assumed, not deduced.

Pure Reason, we perceive, as the mere requirement of coherence, does not tell us what moral values are; and we get no more light from the Kantian conceptions of the Pure Will and the Good Will. Pure will, autonomous will, will devoid of every impulse of sensibility, can be nothing but the will that Reason wills, reason itself in so far as practical, in so far as legislative form; and it gives only this same universality. The conception of the good will adds indeed obligation (action from duty) to universality (respect for law as law); but this has reference only to the case of conflict between respect for the moral law on the one side and the impulses that oppose it on the other. To tell us that it is obligatory to act in accordance with the moral law is not to tell us what the moral law is.

If respect for humanity, or for the human person, as an end in itself, is understood, as it was by Kant, of the rational person, the question remains, whether it is merely the universal reason in each person that is the object of respect, or each personality also in its difference from others.

Only on condition that we conceive the personality as comprising indeed but not exhausting itself in reason, do we get any real content. With nothing but the universally legislative reason to respect in each, clearly, as before, we do not get beyond the form. Respect for the human spirit in the entirety of its manifestations cannot be derived from respect for reason as reason and for law because it is law.

From Kant's own illustrations it is manifest that the reduction of the criterion of moral valuation to a purely formal criterion supposes the ends of moral action already known as to their content; duties already known and determined as to their object. An answer is given to the question, When is the intention of the action truly good, when is an act truly moral? but not to the question, What are the actions into which this good will ought to translate itself, what are the ends to which the good will ought to turn? In short, the question is not answered, What are the *values* in the effecting of which with purity of will morality consists?

The answer is in fact given by the moral conscience. But what if the answer were equivocal? Suppose that in two consciences there is equal respect for the moral law, but that the law commands to one what it forbids or does not command to the other. Is the opposition got rid of by the knowledge that the will is good when it is determined by respect for the law, and that morality consists in fulfilling duty for duty's sake?

2. *The Diversity of the Moral Criteria.* There are in truth as many moral consciences as there are personal consciences in which certain values are recognised as supreme and normative and valid independently of the momentary and variable flux of transitory and accidental valuations; and as valid alike for one's own judgment and will and for the judgment and will of others. The singular fascination exercised by the ethics of Kant comes not from the formalism in itself, but from the faith that beneath the form there is only one content, the same for all consciences that are moral. All efforts to prove this, however, are vain. The demand of reason for coherence in the sense of consistency can indeed be rigorously maintained; but it is an illusion to think that rationality by itself suffices to distinguish values from non-values, moral values from non-moral values; that it can make us recognise the value of any object, ideal or real, without recurrence, direct or indirect, to some non-rational datum or postulate.

To take examples: the devotee of money, the devotee of art, the devotee of knowledge, can all regulate their thoughts and actions with equal rationality by applying consistently to their own lives and to those of others their own estimate of the highest good. And, while moral values, as has been shown, cannot be reduced to heterogeneous values,—hedonistic (egoistic or altruistic), noetic, aesthetic or religious,—yet all the modes of life connected with these various values do in fact take upon themselves an ethical form; the dominant value being applied universally as a test.

At the same time, diverse as they are, they all recognise, though in subordination to their supreme end, certain moral virtues commonly so-called, such as temperance, force of will, veracity[1]. So again, the man whose distinctive interest is moral, the *homo ethicus*, has to recognise in artistic, religious, intellectual, economic values a direct or indirect moral value. Further, applying the consideration of "organic value" felicitously brought out by G. E. Moore (*Ethics*, chap. vii. p. 246), viz., that "the amount by which the value of a whole exceeds that of one of its factors is not necessarily equal to that of the remaining factor," we find that the ideal object of the moral valuation may acquire a greater value when knowledge or sense of beauty is added, though these are regarded as in themselves diverse interests[2]. It is not without significance that the highest good has been identified with the highest truth and the highest beauty. Moreover, the

[1] This observation reappears in the next section in a more generalised aspect.

[2] Cf. Moore, *Ethics*, p. 247: "Whatever single kind of thing may be proposed as a measure of intrinsic value, instead of pleasure—whether knowledge, or virtue, or wisdom, or love—it is, I think, quite plain that it is not such a measure; because it is quite plain that, however valuable any one of these things may be, we may always add to the value of a whole which contains any one of them, not only by adding more of that one, but also *by adding something else instead*."

A particular case of "organic value" is stated by Hume in the *Treatise of Human Nature*, Book II, Part iii, sect. 10, "Of curiosity, or the love of truth," where he shows how the addition of even a small degree of philanthropy makes an immense difference to the love of truth as a passion.

consciousness of the *homo ethicus*, coming to recognise in morality the internal notes of spontaneity, liberty, autonomy, as distinguished from mere external conformity, is led to extend the intrinsic dignity of moral values to the other spiritual values also which have these notes.

Thus the present situation is that, for the general uniformity of content that prevailed in European morals approximately from the triumph of Christian ethics[1] to Kant, there has substituted itself a variety of systems recognising different criteria of value. The systems differ not, as before, by proposing different foundations for a common content, but by expressing, perhaps in their larger or more significant part, a diversity of contrasting contents. And the common content still recognised has for the personal conscience no greater authority in itself than that of the content marking out the particular system. There seems no issue then unless the conscience itself can or must recognise, without abandoning its own criterion of valuation, some difference, if not of kind then of degree, between one valuation and another.

3. *Conditionality in the Moral Values.* Let us make the improbable supposition that the philanthropic, the speculative, the religious, the aesthetic spirit, recognise no values at all save those that can be measured by the criteria of their own ideal ends. Even so, it will be

[1] This means, more generally, the ethics of later antiquity, predominantly Stoic, which largely passed over into Christianity. The political conditions of the ethical modifications noted by Juvalta were the transition from the city-State, with its vigorous self-affirmation of diverse types, to the uniformity of an imperial civilisation, and then the return, after the dissolution of this, to varieties based in independent but interacting new nationalities.

found that certain endowments, for example, promptitude, tenacity, self-control, courage, are and must be considered as values by all the types without distinction; because all, if they are intelligent, must recognise in these personal qualities conditions either indispensable or extremely useful for the realisation of the order of values peculiar to each. For the same reason, it will be found also that respect for the inviolableness and liberty of the person, observance of contracts, exchange of services, and the customs, institutions, laws and dispositions of spirit connected with them, such as probity, impartiality, sympathy, must be recognised as values. All the types therefore will be led to recognise and appreciate in themselves and others—abstraction made of every moral valuation— values personal and social that arise out of this relation of conditionality with respect to all alike. Since this is a necessary and permanent relation, each of the types must recognise in such values a certain precedence over the direct and final values that depend on them.

We arrive thus at the distinction between those conditioning values for which every conscience can recognise as legitimate an external legislation imposing them, and the final values of which an external legislation ought merely not to exclude the possibility. For the former are conditions for all, while the latter are, by the hypothesis, values each only for its own type[1].

The examples adduced so far do not, however, correspond to a rigorous determination. If we try to fix with precision the values that make up this common content, we shall find that they are summed up in two conditions

---

[1] The very exclusiveness of each type is thus made to compel generality if they are to live under a common system.

recognised in effect as primary fundamental values by every moral system: namely, liberty and justice. These conditions emerge when each type—the philanthropist, the speculative inquirer, the mystic, the artist—recognises both that it cannot carry its positive imperative beyond the common values and that it must *not deny* the orders of value that give direction to the other modes of life; that none is entitled to impose its peculiar criterion on the others as the ultimate test.

To bring to actuality in oneself and in every other person these values of liberty and justice, and the values implicit in them, must be recognised as a duty universally valid; or rather as the only duty, or the only category of duties, truly universal.

But liberty is not a condition that exists in fact, a given possession; it is a conquest to be made, an ideal that requires ever new efforts and imposes ever new duties. And the same is to be said of justice, which is the social mirror of liberty. Also, since liberty and justice have been deduced here as indirect values, there remains always the possibility of a conflict between a direct interest such as that of knowledge or beauty or sympathy, and the mediate and indirect duties of liberty and justice; or, in general terms, between the final values that are supreme for the individual consciousness and the values that appear to it only instrumental.

4. *The Presupposition of every Moral Valuation, and the Fundamental Opposition of the Criteria.* Liberty and justice, however, are not merely indirect moral values, but also values for themselves. To recognise the supreme value, for each, of an end or ideal subordinating all other values and giving a constant direction to the will, is to

recognise the supreme value of that which constitutes the personal unity. Now this implies the absolute value of the human person; for if the personality had no value, the ends and ideals in which it is centred could have none.

This intrinsic and absolute value of the person in itself is the implicit presupposition, the postulate understood in every moral valuation. All discussion on its legitimacy is vain, or rather self-contradictory. By this presupposition, it is imposed on me that I should be a person and should will that every human being should be a person; and not merely a human person as rational being in general, but this particular person. Distinctive personality, expressing itself in an ideal, coincides with liberty in the positive sense. The recognition of its value in others is the demand of justice[1].

The proof that the end chosen is the end of a coherent personal will and not a mere caprice of the transitory and mutable ego is the readiness for sacrifice. The value of life is measured by the value of that to which one is ready to sacrifice it.

The moral value of the particular content of the will springs from its being the means by which the absolute value of human personality expresses itself in the individual consciousness. Thus the ideal in which the criterion or the law of moral valuation embodies itself for the conscience of individual persons constitutes for each the affirmation of the spiritual unity of its will to be a person, of its liberty. And so liberty, which before

[1] These two points, not stated here by Juvalta in so many words, but formulated below, seem to me to constitute the nerve of the argument.

appeared only as a common condition for actualising every
order of values, becomes here a value by itself immediately
universal and at the same time proper to the individual.
The imperative of liberty is at once: Be a person, and
Be thyself; Respect humanity, and Respect in thyself
and in all others the individual and concrete expression
of humanity.

This does not mean of course that there is a duty to
be original as well as to be just; though each personality
has its shade of difference that should aim at expression.
The individual differences, however, group themselves
around certain types, and hence arise necessary oppositions. The fundamental form of opposition, which
criticism can only establish and not get rid of, is the outcome of the contrast between the universal moral values—
the values of liberty[1] and justice—and those that have
supreme value for the individual consciousness. Briefly,
the antithesis is between the values of justice and the
values of culture; between the requirement that each
should be or should have the power to become a person,
that is, a free, conscious and coherent will, and the requirement that he who is already a person, that is to say,
who has the consciousness of his duty and power to make
himself free, should augment and enrich himself by new
values. It is the antithesis between number and quality,
between extension and intensity; between the duty of
rendering those participators in the values of liberty who
are not already participators, and the duty of increasing
in those who already possess them the values of culture,

---

[1] Here of course liberty means the equal liberty of others, not the
liberty of the particular personality in question, which is identical with
the effort towards its own ideal end.

which are, at least mediately, an increment in the values
of liberty.

Are the two paths convergent? Let us hope that they
are; but at present the question is to determine which is
the predominant moral requirement: the increase of a
culture from which most of those who are its necessary
instruments are excluded, or the removal or diminution
of this exclusion.

To say that the culture of the few is necessarily the
elevation of all, or that the elevation of all is necessarily
increase of culture, is to delude oneself with words; it
is to repeat in another strain of optimism the old-fashioned
coincidences of the general good with the individual good.
Saying so does not make it so.

5. *The Relations of Morals to Politics and Religion.*
Politically an opposition of tendencies displays itself in
different conceptions of the justice constitutive of the
State. To the universal moral values corresponds an
obligation at once external and internal; to the properly
personal moral values, an obligation only internal. This
is the general position, determined by the ideal that the
State, considered ethically, has to realise; but there are
different views as to the precise character of the justice
that should fix and preserve the conditions necessary for
the liberty of all. Thus we find the interest of diversity
defended by a relatively conservative Liberalism; while
strictly equal external possibilities for all to become
persons are championed by that which is wrongly called
Socialism, but would rightly be described as Universalistic
Individualism. Under the actual conditions, this difference issues in a conflict juridical in form and economic in
substance.

Now it is to be noted that if for the contest of higher interests (noetic, aesthetic, religious or altruistic) so far considered, we substitute interests of egoistic hedonism, we arrive at precisely the same universal values of liberty and justice; provided only that the egoist will rationalise his egoism, that is to say, will recognise that in the same conditions the same criterion of valuation is admissible for all. And in fact we find that political liberalism, in its purely political, that is, external aspect, is modelled on the conception of economic freedom. This only in appearance contradicts the thesis that a value cannot be normative unless considered as distinct from the transitory and variable desires of the subject; for the value contemplated by economics is not pleasure, or subjective satisfaction, but wealth, which is a common term of reference for all hedonistic values, being the instrument for attaining them in general. So far as method is concerned, the norms of justice can be most simply deduced from the egoistic conflict formulated in economic terms.

Hence follow two corollaries. The first is that the political power, so far as coercive, that is, acting by sanctions and therefore appealing to egoistic motives, is not in itself an organ of morality: political institutions are moral or immoral only as inwardly estimated by the individual conscience. The second is that, since the juridical order has to justify itself from an egoistic point of view, it must consider the higher goods first only as hedonistically desirable. Having thus brought them under the class of values desired for the sake of hedonistic satisfaction, it can then proceed to fulfil its ethical or educative function, which is to promote culture by

preparing the conditions necessary for rising to the effort
after these higher goods.

When the State is considered in relation to other
States, it assumes the nature and function of a Person
among Persons. Here we come upon an antinomy in
the relations of the citizen and the State, according as
the State is considered in its internal action or in its
external conduct. In the former relation, the political
Power is from the ethical point of view the means and
the single person the end; in the latter, the State is end
and the citizen means. The political parties that consider
the opposition of States as insuperable and the sovereignty
of each State as ethically unconditioned tend to make the
second order of conceptions prevail. Those that believe
that the opposition can be overcome and that the
sovereignty of States in their mutual relations is ethically
conditioned manifest the opposite tendency.

The individual modes of life directed by an ideal
have a resemblance to a personal religion; and, if we
conceive the moral ideal as realised in a Being whom we
call God, our devotion to the ideal becomes actually
religion. There is consequently a certain analogy between
the relations of morals to religion and to politics. The
political Power realises the external conditions of morality;
the divine Virtue, conceived as the spring of all ideals,
realises the internal conditions. Since the realising of the
moral value in action consists essentially in an act of will,
which is internal and spiritual, and material and external
conformity derives its value from that, the political
Power may then appear to the religious conscience as if
it were the means and instrument of the religious Power.
This view, however, is corrected for the religious

conscience itself when it is brought to recognise that the external legislation finds its justification in that same fundamental ethical requirement in the name of which the conscience recognises the supreme value of its own ideal and the divine authority of the Power in which it is fully realised. The requirement consists in respect for the human person as the spring of all ethical value; and implies that liberty which conscience cannot deny to another without making its own liberty an object of contempt.

This separation of the political Power and of external legislation from every particular religious faith, is from an objective point of view not less inevitable than its independence, already noted, of every particular ideal that presents itself as moral. For the certitude of every religious faith is a psychological certitude in the person holding it. But to recognise this inward and personal character by which a faith is at once indemonstrable and beyond the reach of external criticism, does not strip the various faiths and ideals of the tendency to deny and exclude their opposites. This very diversity of valuations, each claiming universal validity, is the source of all increase of culture and of all spiritual elevation. It is the values for which the political Power stands, the universal moral values of liberty and justice, that impose limits on the conflict. In relation to the dignity of man, which consists in the affirmation of his spiritual aims, liberty comes before life. *Liberum esse hominem est necesse; vivere non est necesse.*

CHAPTER VI

ABSTRACT AND CONCRETE ETHICS

The advance of Juvalta's ethical doctrine on Kant's seems to me to be twofold. On the one side he reaches a higher degree of abstraction, clearing the idea of moral law even in appearance from all association with external command. On the other side he more expressly recognises the necessarily empirical character of all ends. What is still needed is the recognition that the doctrine founded is not, even potentially, the whole of ethics according to the historical conception of ethical philosophy, but ethics in a certain aspect; Abstract Ethics as distinguished from the Art of Life in general. From this again, if we regard Abstract Ethics as an existent doctrine, we must distinguish Applied or Concrete Ethics, which is the Art of Life in so far as considerations of Abstract Ethics determine modifications in actual conduct. By these distinctions (recapitulated from Chapter III) the objections that might be raised to the incompleteness of the guidance offered towards human good are met beforehand. We perceive that this in its fullness is an affair of innumerable sciences and arts, each to be pursued by its own adepts; and that ethics proper, as has been said, is no more than a kind of logic of conduct. This cannot enter into all the detail of what we ought to do, any more than a text-book of logic can properly become an encyclopaedia of human knowledge.

Concrete Ethics, as it has existed historically, is a fluctuating subject. What is most conspicuous in the classical works on ethics is the extreme variety and the mixture of points of view. Since in principle the whole Art of Life was included, and the limited doctrine called Abstract Ethics was not usually distinguished under a special name from the rest, there had to be selection from an infinite subject-matter. This has been more or less arbitrary, and often determined in later times merely by the established tradition of discussing certain things and not others. One method of selection, which was especially that of antiquity, is, under the direction of a certain end conceived as the highest good, to map out a mode of life for philosophers. Here especially we see the resemblance to religion, noted by Juvalta, of any life according to an ideal. There is no more conspicuous example of this than Epicureanism as presented by Lucretius at the opening of his sixth Book. Epicurus is celebrated as the Teacher of all truth—

> Cuius et extincti propter divina reperta
> Divulgata vetus iam ad caelum gloria fertur,

who found mortals, after they had attained all material goods, suffering inwardly from the sense of sin, and showed them the narrow way that leads to the highest good:

> Veridicis igitur purgavit pectora dictis,
> Et finem statuit cuppedinis atque timoris;
> Exposuitque bonum summum, quo tendimus omnes,
> Quid foret, atque viam monstravit, tramite parvo
> Qua possemus ad id recto contendere cursu.

But this good, though the good of all, it is clearly

seen, will be sought only by a few. And so approxi-
mations to it are usually admitted; as indeed also by
religious teachers, who, recognising that the mass of
mankind will not attain sanctity, yet have something to
say to them. Thus with the Stoics there is the possibility
of making progress to an end perhaps unattainable;
with the Neo-Platonists there are the civic virtues for
those who cannot reach intellectual vision or mystical
ecstasy; and, long after, Spinoza renews this last distinction in another form.

Now it is interesting that Comte and Mill, pre-
eminently teachers who ground themselves upon experience, and at the same time seekers of a good for all,
have more in common with this attitude of primary
appeal to an exceptional few than teachers like Spencer[1]
or even Kant, whose bias is to abstract deduction.
Spencer in particular seems to have regarded philosophy
simply as a profession or employment like any other,
which merely happened to be his own. Thus we arrive
at the result, perhaps unexpected, yet, it seems to me,
quite prepared for and explained by Juvalta, that the
doctrines of the end or of the good are more esoteric than
the doctrines of law. This is as it should be if the good
for different types is various. Abstract ethics then becomes a kind of impersonal science of the conditions under
which all the types are bound to live in common. And
the variety of the types is of course not exhausted in
the philosophic systems of morals. It must be recognised,

[1] Of all the great English experientialists, Spencer, it is generally
recognised, comes nearest to philosophic rationalism. And as, in
common with Hobbes, he had a stronger system-building impulse than
the others, so also he is to be classed with Hobbes in so far as he at least
attempted a doctrine of Abstract Ethics.

on the same general principles of liberty and justice, that the artist, the man of letters, the politician, the man of the world, the man of business, are all entitled to their own manuals of conduct. But evidently none of these could become manuals for schools; and no more can ethical doctrines of the good. To follow with intelligence discriminations among the kinds of goods requires relatively mature experience. To follow the outlines of a fairly easy abstract deduction does not. Hence, apart from its interest among the philosophical sciences, the special province reserved for abstract ethics seems to be that of furnishing the basis for moral education under the conditions of the modern State. This was very clearly perceived by Renouvier, who, from the starting-point of his own Kantianism, went some way towards fulfilling the demand for a popular and teachable doctrine. That Comte's or Mill's doctrine could not equally well have furnished this basis ought to be evident at a glance. It is precisely the abstract character of the moral law that adapts it to be taught first, like geometry in a scientific curriculum. And the doctrine of the good, apart from the theoretical objection to it if it claims to establish by itself the supreme norms of conduct, cannot be made an affair of abstract deduction. Nor can it, of course, like the beginnings of the physical sciences, be made an affair of easy experiment.

Renouvier's contention, that no doctrine of the good, however elevated, can, in the absence of *a priori* principles of justice, make liberty secure, must I think be admitted[1].

---

[1] This means that I no longer regard my own attempt, in a short paper entitled "The Theory of Justice" (*Mind*, N.S. iv. 99), to find an experiential and evolutionary basis, as pointing the way to an adequate ethical as distinguished from political solution.

It is noteworthy that the ultimate fault which he finds
in the system of Hobbes is not the egoism in itself, but
the theoretical subordination of the law placed over the
individual to an end for the sake of which the law exists.
That this end is only the individual's own good is not the
essential fault, but that it is in the last resort above the
law. Thus the moralists who, against the egoism and
individualism postulated by Hobbes, have brought out
the sympathetic and social factors in morality have quite
failed to establish the essentials of ethics on a sounder
basis, great as may have been the value of their work
in detail. This high opinion of the merits of Hobbes's
solution is quite confirmed by the new development of
Juvalta, whose method resembles that of Hobbes in so
far as he establishes the necessity of the moral law by
postulating a conflict about goods. Where he differs is in
beginning with the goods that are the distinctive ends of
culture, instead of formulating all, as Hobbes did, in terms
of a conflict for power. The more primitive conflict,
however, as we have seen, he brings in at the end in
touching upon the relation between morals and politics;
and he finds the result exactly the same. For higher and
lower oppositions alike, the law of justice emerges as
reciprocal recognition of rights to self-affirmation. The
value of his new method is in showing with special clearness how illusory it would be to imagine that because
in our psychology we have transcended egoism and
individualism we are straightway in agreement about a
common good. Nothing, as he shows, has done more
to make a definite moral rule necessary than the increased
richness of modern life in disinterested ends. For each
of these, by itself, tends to denial of the others. The

most apparently disinterested of all, that of direct altruism in pursuit of the common good, as Renouvier had
already pointed out, does not escape the danger, too clear
in the case of Plato and Comte, of setting up a social
despotism of hierarchs and experts. For if in truth ethics
is an affair of discovering the means to an incontestable
final good, who should be more competent to govern than
those who know?

Of course it is an error on the other side to suppose
that, when once we have our formulae of rights and
justice, all problems can be straightway solved with a
modicum of good will. This has been the error of
revolutionists—an error certainly not too little insisted
on in the century that succeeded the revolutionary age.
My exposition of the Italian thinker must, however, have
made it clear that from this error he is entirely free.
No one could more fully recognise that there is no ready-
made solution of anything, and that, especially in politics,
we have to go by degrees and to work by compromise.
We may regret that the kind of Rationalism we can accept
does not give us quasi-mathematical formulae to be applied
with confidence to all cases by logical deduction; but we
all admit that it does not. And yet we must insist that
the old formulae were attempts to express eternal principles
that can never again pass wholly out of view.

Whatever varying expression they may find, the
principles of "eternal and immutable morality" form the
subject of Abstract Ethics. It is conceivable, though
quite remote from the facts, that these might have no
application in the actual world. This supposition would
be realised if there were no active relations among persons;
if each person could pursue his own good without the

least chance of hindering or helping, or being helped or hindered by, any one else. In that case, the condition of rational action would be simply to construct a scale of goods. The term "justice," if used at all, might be used in the sense suggested by Plato, namely, the performance of its own function by each part of the soul in the relation towards the other functions necessary for the best internal life. Abstract Ethics, or the theory of justice in society and the State, might then be thought out as a subject of intellectual curiosity about what ought to exist if mutual interferences were possible by persons seeking their own good. Its existence would be entirely in an ideal world. But clearly this ideal world, that could be imagined for pastime by self-evolving intellectual monads, is our actual world. A world in which there would be no need for anything but an Art of Life to construct a scale of goods is more remote from all that we know than the world of Abstract Ethics. This therefore, in spite of all difficulty in applying it, is that which gives its practical bearing to the study of moral philosophy.

But of what nature is the application in a world where there is at once co-operation and conflict? This has been partly determined already. On our present view, it is clearer than ever that we cannot work downwards from abstract ethics to all the detail, constructing the moral life as we go on from first principles. The application of abstract ethics is to a life of the pursuit of ends that may be arranged in a scale of goods, but certainly differ for different persons and have fluctuating relations for the same person. On this complex that it did not and cannot create, the ethical norm has to impose limits; and these limits are perceived, when considered, to be strictly

obligatory.   But clearly, on this view, it would be quite
wrong to take as our ever-present aim simply to be moral
in the sense of conforming to the moral law.   For what is
creative in life we must appeal to the principle of love in
the widest sense, and this is spontaneous.   It is this,
psychologically, that must normally give us the impulse
even to be just; but, as justice does not determine our
positive ends, so love does not determine the limit and the
obligation[1].   Complete unification is therefore impossible;
and yet there are not two worlds standing apart.   Between
ends or goods on the one side and law on the other, there
is an intermediate doctrine—or rather there are doctrines
—of Concrete Ethics, varying from age to age.

By way of illustration, I propose to discuss a few
questions of Concrete or Applied Ethics.   If the results
have no particular symmetry, this ought perhaps to be,
as Mr Moore said of some examples in *Principia Ethica*,
a commendation of them to those who are suspicious of
abstract doctrine.

First, what shall we say of the productive and destructive arts that go under the collective names of
Industrialism and Militarism?   Obviously these are in
the main an affair of knowledge and skill working with a
view to ends under tacitly understood conventions.   None
of them could be called in themselves branches of ethics,
and yet they fill a very large portion of life.   The part

[1] That is why Kant insisted so strongly that duty, in the moral
ideal, must be able to subsist independently of affections.   He did not
mean, as was sometimes supposed, that a right action done without
affection or with repugnance is more meritorious for that reason; but
simply that a right action is that which is done, and would be done
with intention, because it is objectively right, whatever the agent's
feelings might be.

assignable to them is probably under modern conditions not less than the "three-fourths," if it does not amount to the "nine-tenths," once assigned to "conduct." Is there then any moral rule generally applicable to them? Some might say that obviously "efficiency" is the supreme rule; but this seems to me, if we are thinking in relation to a permanent social ideal, more than doubtful. The moral rule, consisting in some refinement of justice, would probably apply to them the maxims of the mean and of "nothing too much." Aristotle, from the point of view of the end or the good, discountenanced over-specialism in the acquirement of technical accomplishments, because this was inconsistent with the ideal of the "all-round" man, such as a freeman should desire to become. The same general position might be deduced from the rule of abstract ethics. By that rule, we try to avoid doing in the society of others what we should not wish others to do. Now clearly if every one is to strain after the utmost degree of accomplishment in the lighter things, the amenity of life will be reduced for all. Thus the application of the rule will be, to leave some margin of power unused; and therefore it seems not altogether a blameable form of affectation to affect to do things easily. In an ideal social order it seems to me that this would be carried over to the useful arts. The pursuit of too great efficiency would be avoided in order to leave a reserve of vitality for leisure. Here, we are directly considering the end; but the rule of justice is plainly applicable in the form of the Kantian maxim, not to treat oneself or others as a mere means. For how can any one be treated more as a mere means than by the employment of all his strength in the practice of some useful art?

Of course, as in all things, the existence of a state of declared war modifies the rule. Efficiency then has to become dominant, especially if the enemy has cultivated it both in military and industrial affairs to the highest point. But again, when we turn our thoughts to the state of things after war, we have to remember that, as Aristotle said, war is for the sake of peace; and that strenuous industrialism under armed peace, if no more than that were achieved at the close, would only be another form of war. It would be a form, we must add, in which the nobler competition for the higher goods would be permanently instead of temporarily eclipsed. The ideal of our foes would have conquered.

Even in a state of war, the older ideals of honour and chivalry were an application of a law of more refined justice, and not of efficiency; for they consisted in not using power to the full, in giving the advantage of a conventional rule in case of doubt to one's opponent or competitor and not to oneself.

If, as is possible, these ideals, Greek or romantic, of a world that had emerged or was emerging from barbarism, should ever by general consent be restored in a new form, clearly it is only ways of thinking and feeling enlightened by philosophy that can restore them. No science and no specialism—as the ancients saw clearly enough when there was much less of them—can be anything but instrumental. In the absence of sufficient philosophy, knowledge how to do things may even be pernicious[1].

---

[1] Its compensation comes, if not otherwise, then through the working of the cosmic powers. A world-war, by setting back "dispersive specialism" except as applied to the destructive arts, may do the work assigned by Comte to his priesthood of Humanity, and prepare the way for the renewed influence of general ideas.

On the other side, an ethical view of this kind may become overstrained if applied to action when the condition of conflict is perpetual and no reciprocal moderation can be expected from antagonists. By such overstraining we get the scrupulously faultless persons treated with scorn by Carlyle, and in one typical case condemned by Dante to the vestibule of Hell. After all, the end of action is to produce some effect, and it is sometimes not morally permissible to consider too curiously. The judgment of the world, however, is in the long run lenient to the scrupulous even when they have been rather futile, and is often unjust to those who have pushed devotion to ends to excess without regard for the ethical limit. Apologies are still needed—and still forthcoming—for Machiavelli's abstraction from moral considerations in his discussion of the modes of obtaining and preserving political power. This, impartially considered, seems to be a case in which we may rightly blame the world as it actually was rather than the man. Machiavelli did not invent the methods he analyses, and he does not defend them as just. He nowhere calls good evil and evil good. He simply discusses, without sophistication and with the insight of a practical thinker, what a prince or a people must do for self-preservation and aggrandisement in a world where moral limits are disregarded; and his end was a perfectly justifiable one —the freedom of his country from rule by alien enemies. Here the word "justifiable" may be taken in its strictest sense, as that which was required by justice. The alien enemies were unjust enemies.

Some other apparent conflicts of ideal ends with the most rigorous interpretation of the moral law can be resolved ultimately into conflicts of duties. For example, as Mr F. H. Bradley showed in his *Ethical Studies*[1], the most obvious formula of a moral life is "my station and its duties," interpreted in a rather conservative sense. This, he then seemed to hold, covers most of the ground. Yet, as he also showed, devotion to an individually selected ideal end, even when it involves some neglect or disregard of more obvious duties, cannot be finally condemned as immoral. Kant, discussing what is substantially the same case in the *Grundlegung zur Metaphysik der Sitten*, found it to be in general a duty (given the capacity) to choose the more elevated end—the end of progress in distinction from mere conservation. Not to aim at the higher good would be an actual neglect of duty. The argument of course is from what you would desire that others should do—or not leave undone—in similar circumstances.

In association rather than logical connexion with this topic, the controversy about "art for art" suggests itself. Though now silent, it is still interesting, and it may revive again. The artists who took up the formula seem to have been perfectly right in so far as they insisted that art is one of the absolute values in human life, not reducible to anything else. Their appeal, however, was fundamentally to ethics in a sufficiently abstracted and generalised sense. The "moralists" against whom they appealed were those who had regard only to a very restricted order of values; who were setting up a certain limited social ideal of their time and country, and factitiously transferring to this the feeling of obligation that properly attaches itself only to the eternal and

---

[1] Dating from 1876, and not, I believe, representing in all respects Mr Bradley's present views.

immutable principles. The reason of the antagonism was in fact that the most authorised moralists had no principle but that of the end, and therefore felt bound to see no virtue but in their own type. The more rigorous system can be more liberal. From the point of view of the moral law, the justice of the claim to pursue beauty or truth as an end in itself, when once these ends have emerged consciously, is plain. And here there is a certain symmetry in the positions we have to take up. The artist, on his side, without departing from the aesthetic standard, cannot but recognise the beauty of the moral law; just as the purely speculative thinker must recognise the truth that the moral law exists as an ideal. Of course no actual human being is such a creature of abstraction as to come purely and simply under one of these types; to be moralist, artist or thinker and nothing else: but the points of view exist, and it was important to have them distinguished, and even expressed with some exclusiveness. Only thus could the rights of the different modes of life be established. And the artists who protest against the intrusion of irrelevant moralities ought always to remember that it was Kant, the ethical rigorist, who first gave the philosophy of the Beautiful its distinctive and co-equal place side by side with the philosophy of the True and of the Good.

I now proceed to discuss more circumstantially two questions suggested by Juvalta's brief conclusion on the relation of ethics to politics and religion. I shall take first the question of religious persecution and then that of international ethics[1].

---

[1] I have sometimes called this also international law; but, as will be seen, I have not had in view the existing more or less recognised

On the first question it seems to me that the law of justice gives a perfectly clear decision. The renunciation, in the introductory chapter of Mill's *Liberty*, of any advantage "from the idea of abstract right, as a thing independent of utility," must be itself in turn disclaimed; though this does not in the least deprive Mill's arguments of their value and efficacy. For Mill's appeal is, as he said, to "utility in the largest sense, grounded on the permanent interests of man as a progressive being." And this appeal was exactly adapted to meet the case of those who acquiesced in the policy of repressing certain opinions because they were afraid that if those opinions were to spread the result would be the dissolution of society. Like all the other classical modern defences of intellectual liberty, it was an appeal to statesmen and men of the world. It differs from the appeal of Spinoza for "liberty of philosophising" only by introducing the conception of progress which had in the meantime come decisively into view. Both arguments equally are grounded on the welfare of the State and of human society. In Milton's argument for liberty of the press, it may be noted in passing, there is already an implied appeal to progress; while Locke, in his plea for religious toleration, is content if he can prove it consistent with social and political order. Now some speculative advocates of persecution have put themselves on the same ground. It is undoubtedly for the sake of the permanence and welfare of the State—his second-best State—that Plato elaborates his scheme of an ethical religion taught

customs and conventions among nations, in particular for mitigating the usages of war, but a certain ideal of international morality which can be called "law" because the relations it implies are those of justice.

by authority and maintained by repression of all opinions inconsistent with it.   The root of the historic persecutions, however, was not in misunderstood utility.   The scheme of Plato's *Laws* had no influence on his philosophical successors; and demonstrably it had nothing to do with the actual policy of persecution that dominated Europe later.   Yet that policy, after its decline, has sometimes found retrospective defenders on what we may call in a very general sense humanist grounds.   Joseph de Maistre, a really benevolent man, who wished well to the human race, defended the Spanish Inquisition on the express ground that unity of dogma secured social peace; and his argument for the overlordship of the Papacy was that it represented the ideal of international law over warring kingdoms, and was the only check on misgovernment by monarchs that was consistent with political order.   This of course had been met historically, before it was put forward, by the repeated proofs that insistence on authoritative dogma had been oftener a cause of the dissolution of States than of their conservation; but the reasoning is here of a kind that the champion of liberty can reply to without raising the deeper question of *a priori* right.   Defenders of punishment for opinion who reason in relation to the good of human society can be adequately met on the ground of utility, and could conceivably be persuaded that they were wrong.

This ground, however, if we find ourselves obliged to recognise an *a priori* element in ethics, is not ultimate. And it will not meet every case.   Critical readers have observed that Mill's arguments do not touch "the logical persecutor."   For in fact the logical persecutor does not

aim at any end of human society or of the State, but at
the preservation of a certain dogma as dogma. He wills
that this shall prevail, and he takes the most efficacious
methods; of which the true type was the Albigensian
Crusade followed by the Dominican Inquisition[1]. If you
prove, as Spinoza did, that enforced uniformity of dogma
is not preservative but destructive of commonwealths,
the reply he has in reserve is that a commonwealth may
rightly be exterminated for deviation from the dogma
authoritatively taught by a corporation that is above all
human societies. What reply have we then? The only
adequate reply is that the logical persecutor stands for
direct injustice in the highest things. He is not an
opponent with whom it is possible to reason, but an
"unjust enemy" in a deeper sense than that in which
Kant's phrase can be applied to a hostile nation or
potentate. For, professedly regarding belief in what he
holds for truth as the highest thing in himself, he makes
it his aim systematically to repress the beliefs of others.
If there is injustice at all, it is here; and, if we carry our
ethics into metaphysics, it may be said to be a sin against
eternal justice.

From this, the clearest possible case of the direct
application of abstract ethics, the question of international law differs in being perhaps the most complicated
case. It depends not only on knowledge, but even on
a belief, or the possibility of a belief, that may be called
metaphysical. And yet Kant, who himself pointed out

---

[1] The Spanish Inquisition, as M. Salomon Reinach has shown, is
wrongly taken as typical, for its motives were not purely dogmatic and
its methods were in some respects relatively lenient: see *Cultes, Mythes
et Religions*, ii. 401–417 ("L'Inquisition et les Juifs"); cf. iii. 472–509
("L'Inquisition d'Espagne").

this, regarded it as deducible, certain postulates being granted, from the law of justice. The difficulty of the case will appear if we contrast Kant's view with Spinoza's.

Spinoza did not admit any valid international law or ethics at all; and this seemed to him to follow rigorously from his system, of which the "statical" character is not always kept sufficiently in view. Nations, he holds, are in the "state of nature" with regard to one another. In this state there is neither justice nor injustice, but the rights of all extend as far as their power. Since this is so now, it will always be so; because the universe manifests at all times all degrees of perfection that are possible; and (this seems to be implied) we have no reason for supposing the earth to be better or worse in the kinds of manifestations it offers than any other inhabited globe if such exists. From time to time individuals appear who live by the dictate of reason and succeed in attaining the ideal of "the free man." From time to time also free States arise (democracies or aristocracies or limited monarchies), and these are better than States despotically ruled. When they have come to exist they can be preserved for a period by human wisdom; but the general distribution of types of men and States will not change[1]. Now international law, from this point of view, was an institution in its nature chimerical; and Spinoza puts it in the most precise terms that States simply have no

[1] *Tractatus Politicus*, i. 3: "Et sane mihi plane persuadeo, experientiam omnia civitatum genera, quae concipi possunt, ut homines concorditer vivant, et simul media, quibus multitudo dirigi seu quibus intra certos limites contineri debeat, ostendisse; ita ut non credam, nos posse aliquid, quod ab experientia sive praxi non abhorreat, cogitatione de hac re assequi, quod nondum expertum compertumque sit."

ground of complaint against each other for injustice. Probably he thought it useful to warn a small free State like Holland that it would be mere folly to expect the faith of treaties to be observed when they had ceased to be to the advantage of a more powerful State that had entered into them[1]. This, I admit, is an interpretation developed a little beyond the text; but I think it defends Spinoza from the charge of "immoralism" which has been brought against his doctrine of international politics[2]. It is not immoral to abandon the attempt to realise what we know from the nature of things can never be; and Spinoza thought he had apodictic certainty.

Now Kant's opinion, though this is not obvious on the surface, was not at all that such a view of the universe must be decisively rejected. In fact, he seems to have held it quite possibly true[3]. But, he holds, it cannot be dogmatically asserted. And undoubtedly we should desire, if this were possible, that the moral law recognised within States should be extended to their mutual relations. The end to be desired then is a state of perpetual peace. It is not a duty to believe in the attainability of this; for there is no obligation to hold any belief[4]. The duty

[1] *Tractatus Politicus*, iii. 14.

[2] He himself was one of the apologists of Machiavelli, of whom he says (*Tract. Pol.* v. 7) that, even if we do not know what his aim was, it is reasonable to suppose that so wise a man had some good end in view. Still more may this be assumed of Spinoza; who certainly would not have wished to inspire Bismarck, though it is possible that his teaching on this subject may have had that effect.

[3] There is just as much genuine science in anything as there is application of mathematics; and the reality behind the appearance of final causes may be mechanism. (See *Metaphysische Anfangsgründe der Naturwissenschaft* and *Kritik der Urtheilskraft*.)

[4] *Metaphysische Anfangsgründe der Rechtslehre*, 2 Theil, 3 Abschnitt, Beschluss.

is to act in accordance with the idea of the end, so long as its impossibility cannot be demonstrated. And he held it possible, consistently with what can be demonstrated metaphysically, to believe that through the historical process (supposed teleological) a permanently superior order of political society will be attained as compared with the past. Essentially it is on the ground of such a postulate of progress, inadmissible for Spinoza, that Kant is able to carry the rule of justice into international relations.

Kant's ideal of those relations was not peace on any terms, more especially not under a world-State, but peace among free States recognising one another's equal rights to an independent life of their own. Even a federal world-State he held to be inconsistent with this. His ideal was not federalism, but "federality," which meant fluctuating arrangements among States to keep the peace, but without any central tribunal possessing coercive powers. Schemes of modern pacificists that suppose a fixed organisation like that of a federal union can find no support in Kant. Doubtless he would have thought no international law at all better than a system of this kind; for in an anarchy of States each can fight for its own free existence when threatened, and may find allies; whereas an international organisation strong enough to keep the peace by force would be in effect a world-State. And that, in Kant's opinion, was a sinister dream. International law, in his view, must always remain essentially international ethics, with no sanction except in opinion and feeling and the possibility of forming alliances against aggression. Necessarily therefore the fundamental condition of his "perpetual peace" was that the internal life of each national State must be completely self-directed.

On the whole, I do not think it possible at present to add anything important to the conditions of Kant. The element of abstract ethics in his theory, it may be observed, is this: that the norms which present themselves, after long experience of social and political order, as rules that ought to be observed also between States, are the rules of justice. States ought to recognise one another's rights to existence as if they were equal persons. Now this mutual recognition of personal rights is proper to polities in a general sense republican. Hence only among States republican in this sense (which includes constitutional but not despotic monarchies) does Kant expect the international ideal he has sketched in outline to be permanently recognised. The question then finally is, Can we expect that this republican ideal will prevail? If so, we have grounds for believing in progress towards perpetual peace. Kant believed in it[1]; but the theoretical position he thought necessary and sustainable was merely that it is not metaphysically excluded. His doctrine therefore amounts to scepticism, but a scepticism certainly not unfavourable to action.

Before leaving the subject, it will be interesting to set out briefly Kant's expressions of opinion on the attempt of any single State to continue the method of aiming at union by subjugating other States instead of seeking to live at peace with them. It is the duty of States, he says, since the possibility of this is not excluded, to endeavour to establish permanent peace with one another. To will

---

[1] Kant's faith in the potency of the republican ideal is very definitely expressed in a passage of the *Rechtslehre*, § 52: "Dies ist die einzige bleibende Staatsverfassung, wo das Gesetz selbstherrschend ist und an keiner besonderen Person hängt."

otherwise is to will injustice; for the condition of war is that of injustice. What then, among nations, is an "unjust enemy"? "It is that of which the will, publicly expressed (by word or deed), betrays a maxim according to which, if it were made a general rule, no state of peace among peoples would be possible, but the state of nature must be perpetuated[1]." Under this definition comes the violation of public treaties. This concerns all peoples, whose freedom is thereby threatened, and who are called upon to unite themselves and take away the power of such action from the people that is guilty of the wrong. Yet this does not imply the right to make a State vanish from the earth; for that would be injustice against the people, which cannot lose its original right to combine into a commonwealth; though it may be required to adopt a new constitution unfavourable to the disposition to war.

Some formal qualifications follow; as that in the state of nature, which is the state of war, all are in their degree unjust. "The expression 'an unjust enemy' is in the state of nature pleonastic; for the state of nature is itself a state of injustice." This, however, does not modify the substance of Kant's judgment, which refers to an aggressive return to the state of nature after it has been mitigated by agreements.

In concluding the chapter, a word must be said on a topic which Kant is sometimes blamed for excluding from his ethics altogether. It is undoubtedly true that, in common with other thinkers much influenced by Stoicism, he regards animals, because "irrational," as not properly having "rights." Yet, by drawing certain

---

[1] *Metaphysische Anfangsgründe der Rechtslehre*, § 60.

formal distinctions, he is able to recognise duties "in relation to" animals. It is part of man's "duty to himself" not to weaken sympathetic feeling by cruel treatment of them. In putting them to death, as little pain as possible is to be inflicted; they are not to be worked beyond their strength; and the unnecessary use of painful experiments for the sake of mere speculative knowledge is to be reprobated. "Even gratitude for the long-rendered services of an old horse or dog (as if they were house-companions) belongs indirectly to the duty of man in relation to the animals; directly considered, it remains only a duty of man towards himself[1]."

We may not find this enough: it does not go as far as Pythagoreanism or even as Positivism; but I think in some reports of Kant's doctrine the passage has been left out of view. The general position of his abstract ethics, that animals are to be regarded as means not ends, and therefore as things not persons, has probably effaced a detail that only comes into his concrete ethics. I do not find the position even here quite satisfactory; but Kant's restrictions on the conception of right do not seem to me to follow from the general notion of abstract ethics. The broader view of Juvalta about ends would certainly (though he does not discuss the question) allow a general deduction of maxims of justice, and not merely of benevolence, towards animals. For animals have a resemblance to persons in so far as they are ends for

[1] I cite the passage with Kant's italics, by which he indicates technical distinctions about which he is careful: "Selbst Dankbarkeit für lang geleistete Dienste eines alten Pferdes oder Hundes (gleich als ob sie Hausgenossen wären) gehört *indirect* zur Pflicht des Menschen, nämlich *in Ansehung* dieser Thiere, *direct* aber betrachtet ist sie immer nur Pflicht des Menschen *gegen* sich selbst" (*Tugendlehre*, § 17).

themselves though unconsciously. Their "supreme end" we may call self-conservation, including the "values" involved in feelings of vitality and pleasures of perception. Hence they ought to be treated with something resembling the regard paid to persons. They may be considered as having a *right* not to be unnecessarily injured or thwarted in their natural activities.

Whether it would make much difference actually if they were considered only as subjects of benevolence I do not know. Comte, who did not recognise "rights" but only "duties," gives an important place to the domestic animals as a subordinate portion of the great organism which is Humanity. And, in a speculation at the end of the *Tugendlehre* on the constitution of the universe, Kant himself throws out the conjecture that Love must be conceived as creating the world and Justice as only the limiting condition[1]. This he regards as lying beyond the bounds of ethics and leaving for reason an insoluble problem. Yet, before meeting with the passage in Kant, I had arrived at the idea not in this transcendent sense, but as a possible formula for the life of Humanity. I have already put it, as it presented itself to me, in discussing the relations of End and Law. The result seems to be that the active thing in conduct is always in some form love directed to an end. If then in one sense the law is supreme, in another sense the end is supreme. In life it is probably best, whenever it is possible, that the end should be consciously and the limit unconsciously realised.

---

[1] In this "Schlussbemerkung," Eternal Justice is described as not really personal, but only personified in the theistic conception, and is compared to the Fate of the ancient philosophical poets.

CHAPTER VII

METAPHYSICAL CONCLUSION

At this point, if we are to make progress, it seems to me necessary to diverge from Kant. By the method of the *Practical Reason*, nothing can be done in metaphysics. I am one of those who, after reading the more subtly speculative passages there and elsewhere, find themselves led to the conclusion that the theological positions laid down by Kant, so far as they coincide with ordinary theism, are exoteric. Indeed he tells us this himself sometimes almost in so many words. What is essentially unsatisfactory in his procedure is that, after setting forth evidently with the deepest conviction "the autonomy of ethics," he appears to be justifying his ethical doctrine retrospectively by a theoretical doctrine which we are to choose, as against another equally possible, simply on the ground of the ethics. And yet he himself, as we have seen, admits that no belief is obligatory. To try to defend all this, with whatever skill it may be done, can lead only to fresh perplexities. No further insight is attainable within the system.

The new departure I propose is to treat the ethical

doctrine arrived at as established, and as needing no
foundation outside ethics; to admit nevertheless that it
raises metaphysical questions beyond itself which, if we
were not moral beings, we should not put; and then to
seek the answer to these as questions of speculative
truth. That is, we again treat them as ontological
questions: but we acknowledge that the terms in which
we ask them could not have been primarily derived from
any intellectual determinations of pure being; and that
the Kantian analysis has enabled us to understand much
better our own meaning in asking them.

First, however, we must know clearly what can be
arrived at before any question is put that involves ethical
terms. And here I think we cannot do better than recur
to Hume and then find if anything is added or taken
away by Comte. Metaphysical positions, if such exist,
that are left standing by Hume and Comte seem not
unlikely to prove indestructible.

The metaphysical positions we are now interested in
relate of course to the order of the whole, and not merely
to "theory of knowledge."

Now Hume, in the *Dialogues concerning Natural
Religion*, not directly applying the sceptical results of his
philosophy, but proceeding on the commonsense assumption that the external world is known to us as a collection
of material objects, set himself to examine the customary
arguments for theism and to discuss the philosophical
objections to them. With such dialectical skill was this
done that it remains impossible to determine from the
Dialogues whether Hume was in opinion a Theist or not:
the drift of the arguments is completely sceptical. Yet
one position—not amounting to anything that can be

called Theism in the ordinary sense—remains as the residue: "*That the cause or causes of order in the universe probably bear some remote analogy to human intelligence.*" Hume is quite clearly committed to this, though he tries, with his constant determination to give sceptical colouring, to minimise its importance. And, if we return from the more popularly-written *Dialogues* to his radical philosophical work, no less a residue necessarily remains after all the destruction of dogmatisms. For the external world is according to Hume (here continuing Berkeley) phenomenal, that is, an appearance for mind; and if even the "spirits" of Berkeley do not survive, but mind also as substance or unity is dissolved after corporeal substance has vanished, the disaggregated fragments that are left, being "particular perceptions," are still mental. Any philosophy whatever, that could be constructed by starting with this residue as a new beginning, would therefore necessarily imply a resemblance—doubtless remote—of that which is ultimate in the causation of what we call nature to human intelligence.

The expression is well known in which Comte described Atheism as "the absurdest of all theologies." This has sometimes been taken for a mere formal repudiation of an unpopular name by a declaration of agnosticism as against the profession to know things in their reality. We know only phenomena, not their "causes," and our knowledge is "relative." It is true that Comte usually gives the impression of being at bottom sure that the world is of the nature of an object in which, apart from the life of men and animals, intelligence has no part. Yet, if we look closely into some few speculative passages, we find that the declaration

8—2

quoted, so far as it refers to mechanical atheism, is much more than formal. For Comte's analysis of mechanicism is very exact. He treats it, considered philosophically, as the doctrine in which, from the "hylozoism" of the early Greek thinkers, the subjective notion of something resembling life and intelligence in the material elements of the world has been eliminated. This hylozoism itself he regards as a derivative of "fetishism," or the primitive theory that all things are animated by intelligent wills. In Comte's view this is the earliest of the "theologies," which are attempts, prior to objective science, to make a synthesis from the point of view of the subject. It is not only the earliest, but the most plausible, and not the least rational. It is the doctrine by which, in the final stage of philosophy and religion, poetic imagination will still be inspired. And, though known for fiction, it will have this advantage, that it is really a synthesis, though "subjective." An objective synthesis, on the other hand, a synthetic view of nature dependent solely on principles of science, is necessarily impossible; for science, to be effective, has to deal with phenomena in their abstract aspects, never as a totality. Taking this view, clearly he was fully entitled to say what he did about mechanical atheism as an attempt at ultimate explanation. Hylozoism is plausible because it begins with the elements of both object and subject. Mechanicism, considered as an "absolute" doctrine, and not merely as method in a portion of the sciences, is devoid of all plausibility because it rejects what is a part of every appearance, and then tries to explain the rejected part by means of the rest. In one passage Comte goes further, and definitely asserts, as any idealist might, that if there were no intelligence anywhere, no subject as distinguished from object, there would be no real world at all[1].

The basis of intelligence as known in our experience is life; hence for our world to be a real world at all it was necessary that life should exist. Cosmology and biology imply one another. As a science, in Comte's view, biology is necessarily teleological; and, knowing in detail (as many biologists do not) what mathematico-mechanical explanation means, he held this character to be incapable of resolution into anything else. There is no possibility of expressing the nature of life in terms of mechanism. Each higher science, while it depends on the lower, introduces a new principle necessitated by the new complication of its phenomena. Thus, while physics and chemistry form the necessary basis of the sciences of life, the simplest vital phenomenon cannot be expressed in purely physico-chemical terms. And this does not mean (as Kant might have said) that biology in so far as it is non-mathematical falls short of being a true science. The immanent purpose of an organism, the coordinated direction of its activities to ends, is a strictly scientific conception, and must be held the permanently distinguishing notion of biology in the series of the abstract sciences[2].

---

[1] *Système de Politique Positive*, t. i. p. 439: "Il existe, sans doute, beaucoup d'astres incompatibles avec tout organisme, animal ou même végétal, comme le sont, dans notre monde, les corps dépourvus d'atmosphère. Mais notre planète fût-elle, contre toute vraisemblance, la seule habitée, il faut bien que la vie et la pensée se développe au moins là pour concevoir sans contradiction la moindre existence réelle. En un mot, tout phénomène suppose un spectateur; puisqu'il consiste toujours en une relation déterminée entre un objet et un sujet."

[2] Such a distinctively scientific mind as Claude Bernard is thought to have been influenced by Comte in the application of this idea to

This portion of Comte's doctrine leads further than he ever came to recognise. Fuller consideration would have shown that a "subjective synthesis," such as that which he planned and partly carried out, may, if its free imaginations are brought under logical conditions, claim for itself truth or the possibility of truth and not mere permissibility as poetic fiction. Incidentally we perceive this when he points out that life does not emerge in a cosmos to which it is only accidentally related, but that in inorganic phenomena there is something preparatory of vital phenomena. "Habit," for example, is not limited to living beings[1]. This is an anticipation of the results of some recent researches. The philosophical consequence seems to be that the inorganic itself admits of no complete explanation from the abstract sciences specially elaborated to deal with it as one aspect of the world[2]. For the facts brought to light—the quasi-organic character of some processes in inorganic things—have been made out by purely experimental research, not as the verification of

physiology. And Littré, averse as he was from Comte's later developments, always continued to hold that teleology must be accepted simply as the mode of law according to which organic phenomena are connected.

[1] *Politique Positive*, i. pp. 606–607 : "En effet, la tendance à reproduire spontanément certains phénomènes vitaux, sans le concours de leurs sources primitives, est essentiellement analogue à la disposition qui fait partout persister dans un état quelconque après la cessation de l'impulsion correspondante. L'unique différence des deux propriétés résulte de la discontinuité des fonctions envers lesquelles la persistance universelle devient l'habitude spéciale. Or, cette transformation n'est point strictement bornée aux corps vivants. Elle se manifeste aussi en cosmologie, surtout quant aux phénomènes du son, dans les appareils dont l'action s'interrompt, et qui reproduisent mieux les effets assez réitérés."

[2] Cf. *Politique Positive*, i. p. 221 : "l'ensemble est seul réel, les parties ne pouvant avoir qu'une existence abstraite."

any mathematico-mechanical formula showing that they were to be expected. Thus their effect is not to suggest that mechanical explanations will sometime exhaust all that there is in phenomena of apparent teleology, but that, for a grasp of the whole, teleology must be carried back into the inorganic.

Too preoccupied with human life to discuss such cosmical speculations otherwise than incidentally, Comte, in summing up the position as regards Theism, substantially coincides with Hume. "Although the natural order is in all respects very imperfect, its production is much more reconcilable with the supposition of an intelligent will than with that of a blind mechanism[1]." The difference here is one of accent. Comte turns his polemical stress against the dogmatic Atheist, Hume against the traditional Theist.

Thus for both Hume and Comte the analogy of the world to a work of human art does not wholly disappear. For Kant, apart from a theology which at least is not for him demonstrable truth, it remains only an analogy. This he definitely states in relation to Hume's *Dialogues concerning Natural Religion*[2]. Nothing is to be asserted as to what the Highest Reality is in itself, but only in relation to the World, which is to be viewed *as if* directed by sovereign Reason[3]. It might therefore be contended (rather in the manner of Hume when he sets against one

---

[1] *Politique Positive*, i. p. 48: "Quoique l'ordre naturel soit, à tous égards, très-imparfait, sa production se concilierait beaucoup mieux avec la supposition d'une volonté intelligente qu'avec celle d'un aveugle mécanisme." It will be observed that my quotations are all from the great work of Comte's later period.

[2] *Prolegomena*, § 58.

[3] This is also the position of Plotinus.

another the positions of the Theist and the Atheist) that all agree: those thinkers who are considered friendly to the theistic tradition admit that there is *only* an analogy; those who are considered unfriendly admit that there *is* an analogy. This, however, would not quite accurately describe the real position of the question. If, as I have argued in the first chapter, an *a priori* or transcendental element (in the Kantian sense) must be recognised in human knowledge, the aspect of the analogy is not quite the same as it is without that admission. The general analogy, with Hume quite indeterminate, points with Comte to the kind of universal sentiency which he allowed himself to imagine as the subject of poetic fictions. With a theory of knowledge modified in the Kantian direction, it points to a different speculative ontology. This speculative ontology is further modified when we allow also an *a priori* element in ethics. If these new elements can be included in the data from which we argue, we are entitled to add successively to Hume's minimum the propositions: *That the cause or causes of order in the universe probably bear some remote analogy to human reason or intellect;* and *That the cause or causes of order in the universe probably bear some remote analogy to human justice.* I will try to show how these modifications are defensible.

The use of the word "cause," it must be allowed, is somewhat inaccurate and popular: what is meant is the ground of order, the metaphysical reality on which the manifestation of order depends. Now the meaning of the transcendental or *a priori* element in knowledge is this: that certain principles, which cannot be derived from mere experience as we receive it, are necessary to constitute experience as a coherent system. This means

VII]   METAPHYSICAL CONCLUSION   121

that the element of "relation" in knowledge, as distinguished from its sensible elements, is as "real" as these; that it is not a mere factitious product of the shifting of the (psychically) material elements. Relations in logic and mathematics and the sciences of causation are not mere blank forms left by the evacuation of deposits from without, but belong to the mind's own activity. But also they are not (as might be inferred from some of Kant's own statements) factitiously imposed on nature by the human mind. What the actual achievements of science prove is that nature shows itself interpretable by mind when mind has the audacity to dictate what its constitution shall be,—provided it combines with this audacity a readiness to immerse itself in facts and change its hypotheses when they will not work.

This view of knowledge enables us to proceed to so much of speculative ontology as has been contended for; but of course we do not pretend to arrive at it without one of those assumptions, called axioms, which are of the very constitution of knowledge. What we have to assume is simply the principle "Nothing from nothing." It cannot be without something corresponding in that from which the mind emerges that there are in the mind applicable principles of knowledge. The human mind as it exists is obviously in some sense a product of a larger whole; hence the principles by which it successfully interprets that whole must be in some way prefigured in the reality of the whole.

Clearly this is just as true for the principles of morals as of theoretical science. Doubtless, as was said, if we had no ethical interests we should not ask why there are principles of morals; but since we are, as a matter of fact, moral beings, the bearing of those principles on the nature of the whole is a speculative question that necessarily presents itself. Thus our result, if valid at all, will be theoretically valid. A metaphysical doctrine that is the response to moral questioning is not of the nature of a decision for the sake of practice, but is the completion of a speculative ontology by means of elements provisionally abstracted from when the human mind was regarded merely as constructing a science of nature.

Man, as we have seen, also constructs a science of ethics, or of what ought to be. In constructing it, he has passed historically to a higher degree of abstraction. Concrete ethics, or the art of life in so far as it is worked out in view of the limiting conditions imposed by morality proper, we found, is related to abstract ethics, or the science of the limiting conditions themselves, as the geometry of antiquity to modern analytical geometry. Here we were able to apply the strict notion of analogy in Kant's sense: the things themselves are not alike, but there is a resemblance of relations. This resemblance of relations depends on the existence of an *a priori* element in morality capable of development to purer detachment, but always present in the human mind since it began to reflect on conduct as consisting in interactions among social beings.

This notion of abstract ethics impressed itself very strongly on Schopenhauer; who was certainly not too desirous of agreeing with Kant, and who, by natural bias, was inclined to look to the end and the concrete case rather than to bring conduct under a system of general laws. Through the recognised necessity of admitting an *a priori* element in morality, he was led to formulate his

metaphysical doctrine of "eternal justice." It is true
that the earlier expression he gives to this, involving the
ultimate illusiveness of the individual, does not answer
any demand ever made by men for justice in the universe :
the important thing was that the demand should be
recognised, even in an ostensibly pessimistic system, as
needing a response. Aiming at no more than the statement of an analogy, I am content at present with this
support for the general argument. I simply argue that
the existence of inexpugnable *a priori* elements in moral
as in natural science entitles us to assert, since nothing
comes from nothing, that not only Reason but Justice in
some sense is a pre-existent reality ordering the constitution of the whole that is partly known to us in the world
and in man.

We cannot, on the ground of this argument, straightway identify Reason and Justice with the Whole of
Reality, or the Absolute. The position indicated is the
Platonic position, in some generalised sense, that "Mind
is King." From this we must not infer the personality
of that which directs the process of the world ; but,
personalised or not, it is this, rather than the Absolute,
when we come to consider it closely and not vaguely,
that corresponds to the theological idea of God.

To trace out the realisation of the order of reason and
justice in the world, a modern mind will look first to its
evolution, physical and organic, and then to the historical
evolution of man. But, if we are to take the idea of
Eternal Justice seriously, these, singly or together, are
insufficient. For eternal justice to have a meaning, we
must affirm what Schopenhauer called the *aseitas* of the
individual, and consider the destiny of this. It would be

unjust, as he insists, if the Destiny that judges had first created by its will that which it is to judge. Nor is each individual to be considered, as sometimes from the point of view of biological and sociological science, simply as an organ through which all the rest of the world acts and which is nothing in itself. It is not a mere complex of hereditary and socially-impressed tendencies, though these contribute to make it empirically what it is; it includes something—that which has not proceeded from anything else—without which the whole world would be different. And perhaps this implies (what I think Schopenhauer does not say) that some individuals are radically evil. This is conjectured to be the meaning of a well-known but obscure passage in Plato's *Laws*[1]. Being thus led to carry forward our speculations to the individual, there is no reason, so long as we can put our questions in intelligible terms, why we should cease to ask them. In the hope of a possible answer we may be led to consider again whether any insight is still to be found in those Greek and Indian theodicies which suppose permanent individualities with lives recurrent in successive ages of the world. The conditions of attempting any new construction with such help seem to me to be a certain freedom of imaginative conjecture together with a constant willingness to bring our imaginations into relation with every kind of demonstrated science. But this lies beyond the bounds of the present Essay.

[1] x. 896 E, with context. What Plato says directly is that some (at least one) soul in the universe must be potentially maleficent, and that this cannot be the soul that guides the whole. I derive the interpretation from Professor Burnet.

INDEX